THE GREATEST AIR ACES STORIES EVER TOLD

The Men of the American, British, and Commonwealth
Air Forces Who Fought for the Sky in Two World Wars

COL. ROBERT BARR SMITH (RET.)

AND LAURENCE J. YADON

D1402258

Guilford, Connecticut

An imprint of Globe Pequot

Distributed by NATIONAL BOOK NETWORK

British Library Cataloguing in Publication Information Available

Library of Congress Cataloging-in-Publication Data

Names: Smith, Robert B. (Robert Barr), 1933- author. | Yadon, Laurence J.,
    1948- author.
Title: The greatest air aces stories ever told : the men of the American,
    British, and Commonwealth Air Forces who fought for the sky in two World
    Wars / Col. Robert Barr Smith (Ret.) and Lawrence J. Yadon.
Other titles: Men of the American, British, and Commonwealth Air Forces who
    fought for the sky in two World Wars
Description: Guilford, Connecticut : Lyons Press, [2017] | Includes
    bibliographical references.
Identifiers: LCCN 2016049499 (print) | LCCN 2016051013 (ebook) | ISBN
    9781493026623 (paperback : alk. paper) | ISBN 9781493029693 (e-book)
Subjects: LCSH: Fighter pilots—Biography. | Flight crews—Biography. | Great
    Britain. Royal Naval Air Service—Officers—Biography. | Great Britain.
    Royal Air Force.—Officers—Biography. | United States. Army Air
    Forces—Biography. | World War, 1914-1918—Aerial operations. | World War,
    1939-1945—Aerial operations.
Classification: LCC UG626 .S49 2017 (print) | LCC UG626 (ebook) | DDC
    940.54/40922--dc23
LC record available at https://lccn.loc.gov/2016049499

Contents

FOREWORD

THE SKY ABOVE US HAS NEVER BEEN MAN'S NATURAL HABITAT. GRAVITY has made it an unfriendly place since the dawn of time, especially for warriors. And so it remained a mysterious, forbidden world until the early twentieth century, when men first ventured into that uncharted realm above the ground, and did so at first in the most curious collection of ungainly flying machines imaginable. That was not so very long ago, and back then not even the wildest imagination could conceive of jet planes and speeds beyond the velocity of sound.

Yet from the time the first primitive warplane limped off the ground in 1914 to the monumental moment when *Enola Gay* brought the thunder and lightning to Hiroshima was only three decades, a tiny instant in time. The balloon was nothing new, but a structure that provided its own power and went where the pilot directed it to go opened up a whole new dimension of war.

Since then the airplane has become a decisive weapon of war, both strategically and tactically. One of our authors can testify to that: After some time huddling in a minuscule depression in the ground at a hostile place called Dak To, he watched rejoicing as four F-4s dropped their loads of napalm just behind a neighboring ridge that sheltered North Vietnamese mortars. Somewhere in the resulting conflagration the gunners and their tubes fried; there was no more mortar fire. That happy experience has been common among grunts of a number of armies, and no man among them will have anything but praise for his air force.

The tales in *Aces* span the two world wars, although obviously there is much more to write about. And they are largely limited to the pilots of America, Britain, and the British Commonwealth. Two of our most famous enemies appear also. Early on we realized we could not do justice to every flying ace who deserves it in less than a dozen volumes. So it seemed best to write mostly about our own people and our closest allies.

We've also written a little about the planes they flew, the good ones and the bad. There is something about the famous Sopwith Camel, for instance, Snoopy's favorite ride. And the reader will also find out more than he wants to know about the "Quirk," the World War I British BE2c, accurately named by a noted aviation writer as the "world's worst military airplane."

There is something in our book about tactics, and the fickle weather gods, and even the winds, like the World War I Western Front prevailing wind that hampered the ever-aggressive British and American airmen, blowing against them when they tried to nurse a crippled aircraft back to their own lines. We touch on the "scores" of various airmen, although these tallies of enemy aircraft shot down can be misleading. The number of "kills" depends heavily on what equipment the pilots were flying, when they and their country got into the war, how long they survived, and the method of score-keeping.

In both wars, it took a brave man to sally forth day after day in one of the flying machines of the time. This was especially true in World War I, when Allied pilots flew without parachutes. Yet there was never any shortage of volunteers, including men who hated tyranny so much that they volunteered to fly and fight for other lands, long before their own nation became one of the belligerents; a number of those—in both world wars—were Americans.

All of these pilots belong to the ranks of the bravest and the best, and with great respect, this book is dedicated to them, the living and the dead.

BORN OF THE SUN
THEY TRAVELED A SHORT TIME TOWARD THE SUN,
AND LEFT THE VIVID AIR,
SIGNED WITH THEIR HONOR.
—STEPHEN SPENDER

WORLD WAR I

CHAPTER ONE

The Coming of Armageddon (1914)

War came to Europe in the broiling summer of 1914. The spark that lit the inferno was the June 28 assassination of an Austro-Hungarian archduke and his wife on a visit to Bosnia, then a province of the old Austro-Hungarian Empire. The assassins were Serbian, which gave the Empire the excuse to crush Serbia, a chance it had long coveted. While the tragedy at Sarajevo was the spark, the whole dreadful mess had been building for many years, and Europe was a system of alliances and pacts and quiet understandings that would bring down the whole house of cards. Old Europe was about to die.

Austria-Hungary issued an ultimatum to little Serbia, deliberately couched in terms so debasing the Serbs could not possibly accept them. And so the continent slid into war, generally with much super-patriotic oratory, pious justification, blaring bands, and shouting crowds cheering on columns of their soldiers marching off to what everybody was sure would be a quick victory.

Britain was not so sure. Perceptive Sir Edward Grey, foreign secretary, clearly saw the abyss opening, and said so:

The lamps are going out all over Europe. We shall not see them lit again in our time.

But no one man, no group of men beyond a few in Berlin and Vienna, could stop the coming catastrophe. And when Germany smashed into little Belgium, the one thing Britain could not tolerate, Britain went to war. The Commonwealth followed, and in time the United States.

In 1914 military aircraft were a rarity. They were, after all, quite new and generally considered unreliable, and got little consideration. After all, virtually all transport and artillery was still horse-drawn, and cavalry, the *arme blanche*, was considered to be the arm of decision. In the first days of fighting, a British cavalry officer was recognized as the first man to kill an enemy with the "new pattern cavalry saber."

But the British did have a few functional aircraft. Like the planes, everything supporting them was makeshift. The mechanics, their spares and tools and tents and such, arrived at Dover partly in commandeered commercial vans, variously labeled "Bovril," "Lazenby's Sauce," and "Peak Frean's Biscuits." The fledgling Royal Flying Corps (RFC)—then only two years old—was on its way to war across the Channel, and its support was going right along any way it could.

The pilots were issued revolvers and rations, and a few brought along their own inner tubes, a sort of meager insurance against ditching in the Channel, a formidable obstacle to the fragile birds of the day. But on the 14th of August, 1914, thirty-seven aircraft of the new Royal Flying Corps left for France, to be greeted with wild enthusiasm by the French population, already terrified at the prospect of "Zeppelin raids," so far creations of the French papers. The RFC had orders to "ram" Zeppelins, not an attractive prospect, but a certain indication of the wild misinformation and fears of the early days of this, the War to End All Wars.

The British aircraft were slow and cranky and unarmed and without radio, but in the first days of the German attack on France and Belgium, they did yeoman service. For the German offensive theory, the carefully tailored "Schlieffen Plan," called for a heavily reinforced right wing to sweep through Belgium, destroying the tiny Belgian army, outflanking the massive French forces farther south, and occupying the Channel ports Britain would have to use to reinforce and resupply its own troops and those of its allies.

The tiny British Expeditionary Force (BEF)—"The First Hundred Thousand"—held that vulnerable flank, and was vastly outnumbered by the German divisions. The British were the finest and fastest riflemen in the world—their standard was fifteen well-aimed rounds a minute—and that lethal musketry inflicted monstrous casualties on the Germans, so heavy that many Germans were sure the BEF had many more machine guns per battalion than the two the British establishment called for.

But the French, with a much larger army than Britain could muster, wasted a vast number of the best of her soldiers in frontal attacks on well-prepared German troops, all in furtherance of a plan authored before the war by a military moron named Grandmaison. The notion was that the *cran* of the French soldier, his courage and *élan*, would sweep everything before it, attacking in closed ranks, wearing his antique red pants and blue coats, roaring "*a la bayonette!*" and similar warlike nonsense. Grandmaison got a great many good soldiers killed for nothing . . . it may have been some small comfort to widows and orphans that ultimately Grandmaison was killed himself.

In the face of great German strength and lack of French help, the British had to fall back, fighting all the way, sore-footed, exhausted, so tired that men went to sleep standing up and hallucinated, seeing vision of angels and columns of cavalry that weren't there. They were ever conscious of the danger of being outflanked. And it was here that the tiny British aircraft contingent proved invaluable; for the British command was seldom blind to what the Germans were doing and where they were.

Had the British been outflanked, they and the French would have been cut off from Paris and the Channel and driven into the interior, and the war would have been all but lost in the first month. But thanks in large part to the British airmen and their antique flying machines, the tiny British command knew where it needed to concentrate and when it needed to move. Their courage and professionalism, and their murderous "fifteen-rounds-a-minute" rifle fire saved the northern flank of the Allies in Flanders. In the end, they and the French fought the Germans to a standstill in what was called the "Miracle of the Marne," and the stage was set for four long, bitter years of war.

The age of the warplane had arrived. In the beginning they didn't carry any weaponry besides the crew's sidearms—a little later, somebody issued boxes of darts to drop on the dreaded observation balloons—and a worse failing was the absence of any sort of radio gear; to pass their vital information to the PBI—British army slang for the "Poor Bloody Infantry"—they either had to find someplace to land, or drop a hastily scribbled message.

Early in World War I, many of the British pilots were young public-school men—little more than boys, some of them—fresh from the playing fields and the classrooms of first-rate institutions. They were the cream of the British Isles, athletes and scholars full of patriotism, idealism, courage, and energy. Many of them could quote Lord Tennyson's magic vision of an age just then being born:

> *Heard the heavens fill with shouting and there*
> *rained a ghastly dew,*
> *From the nations' airy navies, grappling in*
> *the central blue.*

The terrible tragedy was, whether these youngsters started out leading troops down in the mud, or hunting German aircraft "in the central blue," they all too often ended up dead or crippled.

But that is what war does; that is its inevitable price. The bravest and the best, the men most dedicated to their country's good, are often killed or crippled early on and in large numbers. The wonder of it was that they kept coming, going into the inferno again and again; there was, as Kipling wrote, "no discharge in this war."

This book is dedicated to the aviators' memory. The west had seen patriotic young men rally to the colors time and again, before and since. I think they will again. If the day comes that they do not, then everything that is good, all that is noble, will pass away, and the earth will know a new age of foul night. God grant it never comes.

CHAPTER TWO

Only a Broth of a Lad

Albert Ball (RFC)

When England went to war in 1914, the public schools poured out their young men, patriotic, eager, daring to the point of foolhardiness. St. Bee's, a tiny school of only 117 students, produced three Victoria Cross (VC) winners. Men and boys of all social classes joined them, their common bond a fierce love of country. And if all these patriotic men had a model, a single man to emulate, an all-England type, his name would have been Albert Ball.

The son of a sometime mayor of Nottingham who had risen from humble beginnings, Albert was fond of books, paintings, and music, and was a fine writer himself. He was a devout Christian, devoted to his family, an animal-lover and a dedicated Boy Scout, who majored in engineering, and even set up his own minuscule firm, somewhat grandly named the "Universal Engineering Works." But with the outbreak of what Americans called "the Kaiser's War," his thoughts turned to what he could do to defend his England, like so many hundreds of thousands of youngsters like him. And so he enlisted as a private in the infantry, the Sherwood Foresters, today part of the Mercian Regiment. He served in the Nottingham Company, called, not surprisingly, the Robin Hood Rifles.

He rose to sergeant within a month, and quickly made lieutenant, but he remained stuck in England, and he was not at all happy about it, for the war he was eager to fight for king and country was east across the

Channel. The Channel coast was well within the sound of the guns in Flanders, and he was determined to get into the war in any way he could. He had read of the early exploits of the men of the Royal Flying Corps, and that seemed the shortest road to the real war, and so he climbed on his motorcycle and roared off to find his way to a private flying school.

And there he bought his own flying lessons, getting up at 3:00 a.m. to cover the sixty miles to the flying school in time to get into the air at first light, then dashing back to his unit in time for the first formation of the day at 6:30. The learning process was punctuated by two serious crashes, and Ball's evaluations were not high, but still he persevered until he got his civilian license.

At last, after wading through much government red tape, he finally got his chance and a commission, and was posted to an RFC line squadron in France in February 1916. While Ball was delighted the assignment was not all good, for his squadron—number 13—still flew the BE2c, known to all as the "Quirk," notorious as the worst aircraft of this or any other war. Its unpredictable, malevolent nature deserves a word or two.

Stories about this eccentric flying farce abounded. There was a tale that it "blew off its cylinders in the order of firing," and flew *backward* in the smallest head-on breeze. It was ungainly; one World War I pilot referred to it as a "flying grape arbor," and it was mechanically cranky. It sometimes fought gallantly on, even staying in the air while shot to pieces, but on other days it would crash without a shot being fired. Some Quirks sported a peculiar forward-firing machine gun—well, not exactly forward—it was mounted on a peg on the fuselage, so that the pilot could shoot at an angle *generally* forward, sort of kittywampus to avoid the arc of his own propeller.

The best story of all was of the Quirk that caught fire, obliging her two-man crew to climb out on the leading edge of the wing and sit there. And then this obliging airplane rammed a German balloon and set it afire, and finally on her own motion landed safely on the back of a British truck headed to the rear.

Well, maybe, or maybe that's pure mythology, but the Quirk was indeed famous for the unexpected and inexplicable . . . and one thing she did that paid for all her faults: She was part of the eyes of the British army, the vigilant eagles whose reports to the tiny British Expeditionary Force tracked the German juggernaut on its way west across France in the summer of 1914. That up-to-date intelligence contributed in a major way to the "rally on the Marne" that stopped the Germans cold. Much of what she did right she owed to her aviators, for of nineteen Victoria Crosses won by the Royal Flying Corps, three went to Quirk pilots. And most remarkable, over a thousand Quirks were still flying when the war ended in 1918.

Ball cut his teeth on so-called secret missions, flying intelligence agents into hostile territory and dropping them off in pastures or any-place else a lumbering biplane could land. Most agents were brave, patri-otic French or Belgian men, but there was the occasional case of cold feet. Ball was having none of that, and when one of his passengers lost his nerve when the time came to leave the airplane, Ball forcibly jerked him out of the aircraft, shoved him toward a nearby hedge, and flew away.

He flew artillery "shoots," as well, observing the effect the Royal Artillery's pieces were having on the enemy, and sending back corrections to the gunners. This unglamorous mission was vital to the PBI. He some-times flew the artillery-spotting runs under German fire, and at times when the weather was vile, so bad that many of the artillery spotters did not come back from their missions. Whatever Albert Ball was sent to do he gave the job everything he had, but always his warrior's soul longed to be about the business of combat.

At last Ball got his opportunity to fly a single-seat fighter—initially a Bristol Scout—but victory in the air eluded him until the summer of 1916, and the bloody Battle of the Somme. His first kills were an enemy balloon and a Roland two-seater—he felt sick watching the German crew going down in flames, but it would not stop him. He still flew almost constantly, cultivated a little flower garden in what time he could spare, and sometimes played his violin in the mess at night.

German observation balloons—the *Drachen*, "dragons" in German army slang—were a source of many Allied casualties from accurate artillery fire, and therefore high on the list of targets for the men of the RFC. They were not soft targets, for they were surrounded by heavy concentrations of anti-aircraft firepower. British airmen, including Ball, went after them not only with machine gun tracers, but with something called the Le Prieur rocket, whose incendiary warhead could turn the Drachen into a monstrous torch.

The balloon observers had parachutes, but the canopy was in a pack secured to the side of the balloon's basket. An observer simply jumped over the side if his balloon was hit and the chute opened . . . that is, if the fiercely blazing Drachen didn't follow him down, as sometimes happened. Ball had several balloons to his credit, and perhaps that added to the stress he began to show.

In October of 1916 Ball was posted back to England. He had thirty-one confirmed kills by this time, was promoted to captain, and had won the Distinguished Service Order (DSO) and the Military Cross (MC). He was the leading British ace and was much honored by his friends and neighbors in Nottingham. He also became engaged to a charming eighteen-year-old lady who wore Ball's silver identification bracelet in lieu of an engagement ring. But being Albert Ball, he could not wait to get back to the war, and on his return to France was assigned as a flight leader in 56 Squadron, as fine an outfit as there was in the RFC.

Ball got his own hut, up close to the fight line, and with support from General "Boom" Trenchard got his own Nieuport fighter, even though the rest of the squadron had been assigned the SE5, one of the two finest British fighters of the war. Ball worked out an arrangement permitting him to fly the agile Nieuport on his favorite lone-hand expeditions, shifting to the SE when he flew with the rest of the squadron.

He was immediately his old self, a holy terror to the Germans. In one fight he took on a gaggle of twelve enemy aircraft, shooting one enemy down in flames and causing two more to crash, one taking a house with it. Since his fighter had been, in his words, "only hit eleven times," he landed, picked up more ammunition, and took off again to attack a flight of some fourteen Germans, some fifteen miles on the enemy side of the front. This time it did not go so well. As Ball wrote his family:

My windscreen was hit in four places, mirror broken, the spar of the left broken, also engine ran out of petrol. But I had a good sport and good luck, for I was brought down about one mile over on our side. Oh, la, la. Topping, isn't it?

"Good sport" indeed; "topping," surely. The old public school spirit was showing bright and clear. Ball's attitude was typical of young British pilots, whose life expectancy was often measured in days. The singing in the mess in the evening reflected their spirit:

Beneath a busted Camel, its former pilot lay;
His throat was cut by bracing wires, the tank had hit his head;
And coughing a shower of dental work,
These parting words he said.
Oh, I'm going to a better land, they binge there every night;
The cocktails grow on bushes, so everyone stays tight;
They've torn up all the calendars, they've broken all the clocks,
And little drops of whiskey come trickling down the rocks.

There were dozens of these lugubrious ballads, and as the evening wore on, there were other verses and other songs more specifically sexual in nature. Their slang for various sexual organs, acts, and postures was virtually limitless.

And for some men their sense of humor never failed, even when the going was not so good. RFC ace Capt. Gordon Bell's exploits included shooting down six Germans in a single day. On one occasion his aircraft was so badly shot up that it would fly only upside down. He made some progress in that unusual attitude, but finally slammed into some unyielding trees. Climbing down from his cockpit, his monocle still firmly in place, he was hailed by a young infantry officer with an inane question, thus: "I say, have you crashed or something?" To which Bell replied somewhat icily, "No, you damned fool, I always land like this."

Ball would have appreciated this story, but at heart his driving motive was to kill as many Germans as possible. It was not sport, although he sometimes wrote as if it were; it was a necessity to preserve his beloved land, a sort of holy war, and when he was over the front hunting Germans, little else mattered. But there is also some evidence that as the long months of danger and strain went by, they were beginning to tell even on Ball the holy warrior. He even told his father that no fighter pilot "who fought seriously could hope to escape from the war." He became sleepy and short-tempered, but he would not let up in his crusade.

In time Ball discovered that he and the SE were made for each other, and after he began to fly the reliable SE, and between April 22 and May 7, 1917, Ball shot down eleven more of the enemy, raising his score to forty-two. He was still the same aggressive, hard-charging pilot, who, wrote an American who knew him, "darted into the attack with the ferocity of a maddened eagle. He would throw himself into the midst of a compact enemy formation and break it up through their sheer fear of collision."

This writer has never seen a maddened eagle, but the metaphor is a good one nevertheless, given Ball's method of attack, simply "going for them bald-headed," in another time-honored British saying. That expression dates all the way back to the Battle of Warburg in 1760, when the English cavalry commander personally led a hell-for-leather charge, routing the enemy but losing his hat and wig in the process.

But at last came the fateful evening of the 7th of May. Ball had spent the rainy overcast day leading a flight from his squadron as part of a much larger formation that beat up an area around Cambrai. Their mission was the typically aggressive British expedition into German territory; just go over on their side and shoot anything hostile that moves, in the air or on the ground, and damn the usual contrary wind that blew from the west.

So it was this day; and as the day wore on and the weather got even cloudier, Ball was last seen as he dove into a bank of cloud, chasing and shooting up a German Albatros fighter. One story says it was the red airplane flown by the Baron's younger brother Lothar, but as will appear the younger von Richthofen could not have fought in this action. Whoever flew it, it became Ball's forty-third kill . . . and his last.

All anybody really knew was that Capt. Albert Ball, the young Lochinvar of the air, had flown into that cloud and had not come back out. He was simply . . . gone.

To this day nobody knows for certain what happened to Ball. He was well known to the German enemy and famous all across the world. Claims were put forward by or on behalf of both the famous Richthofens—the "Red Baron" and his younger brother Lothar—but neither claim can be true. Lothar made the false claim that he shot down Ball's *Sopwith triplane*—both the Nieuport and the SE5 were biplanes, a very obvious difference—and did so on a day when Lothar was in Berlin on sick leave. His more famous brother was also in the German capital that very day.

In contrast to the straightforward, undramatic, casual reports released by the British, such factual distortions by the Germans were not unusual, the better to glorify their heroes in the public eye "for morale purposes." For instance, when German idol Max Immelman was shot down and killed, the official explanation—the propaganda line—was that the Eagle of Lille had shot off his own propeller. In fact, he had fallen to a British gunner, a mundane end that hardly fit the Wagnerian hero image.

The most reliable version of Ball's death comes from a French woman who lived in the town of Annoeulin. She is said to have pulled Ball from his wrecked aircraft and held him in her arms while he died of a massive head wound. The story goes that Ball, being a creature of habit, often flew past the church of Annoeulin and checked the time by the church clock. This time, the Germans, aware of his habit, had put a machine-gunner in the steeple of the church.

There is another version that has him crashing behind the German lines, dead without wounds, maybe the victim of a sort of dizzy spell that had been the end for other pilots; or maybe he was hit by German anti-aircraft fire, as another German suggested.

He was buried in a German military cemetery, and he lies there still. He has a monument—it may still be there—and after the war his grieving father bought the field where his son fell and cemented over the spot of the crash.

Ball was gone, but his memory remained evergreen in the hearts of his family, including his younger brother Cyril, who followed him as an RFC pilot and survived the war. His memory was equally precious to the rest of England, and his parents received his Victoria Cross personally from the hand of King George V. He is remembered in a Royal Mail Stamp, a statue in his native Nottingham, and the Albert Ball VC college scholarships.

Albert Ball would have appreciated all these fine things, but probably even more the verdict of a pilot in his squadron, a man who also fought in Albert Ball's final battle:

I see they have given him the V.C. Of course he won it a dozen times over—the whole squadron knows that.

CHAPTER THREE

Deadly and Ruthless

Mick Mannock (RFC)

THERE WAS NOTHING OF THE IDEALIZED KNIGHT ABOUT MICK MANnock, little trace of the sporting instinct shown by so many pilots of every nation in World War I. Mannock cordially hated the German enemy and made no secret of it. When the fabled Baron von Richthofen fell to a Royal Air Force (RAF) pilot and somebody in Mannock's squadron sportingly proposed a toast to the Red Baron, Mannock would have none of it. "I hope he roasted all the way down," said Mick, according to one account, and he meant every word.

He never lost his loathing of the enemy.

He came by it honestly. The son of an English mother and a hard-drinking Scots-Irish corporal in the Royal Scots Greys, Mannock was born in County Cork, Ireland, in 1887. The family moved repeatedly, wherever the senior Mannock's duty took him, until at last Mannock's feckless father abandoned his family entirely. Mick was only twelve or thirteen, but quit school to help his family and took various menial jobs until he joined his brother Patrick with the National Telephone Company.

The NTC had a contract to lay telephone cable in Turkey, and at twenty-seven Mannock led a crew on this job. But then came the Great War, and he and his gang were thrown into a Turkish prison, Turkey having unwisely allied itself to the kaiser. Mannock was not a docile prisoner, singing British patriotic songs and getting beatings from the guards for his defiance. After he tried to escape, he was thrown into solitary confinement, where his health rapidly deteriorated—from a combination of mistreatment, miserable food, suppurating sores, and dysentery—until the American consul stepped in: The friendly Yankee worked hard for Mannock's release and got it.

When Mick got back to Britain, he was classified as "unfit for military duties," but that was no obstacle to Mannock, a man driven by two of the strongest of motives, hatred and patriotism. By July of 1915 he had rejoined the Territorial (reserve) Royal Army Medical Corps unit of which he had been a member prior to the ill-fated trip to Turkey. He served as a sergeant, but was not content, particularly with one duty he knew he might have to face, treating hostile wounded.

And so in the spring of 1916, he was commissioned in the Royal Engineers. He had acquired an interest in flying, however, and by November he had qualified as a pilot. He was, as other pilots were later to say, "a natural." "He seemed," said one instructor, "to master the rudiments of flying with his first hour in the air and from then on threw the machine how he pleased," and this in spite of being partially blind in one eye, the legacy of a mysterious illness that had left him largely blind for a period of weeks.

By April of 1917 he was in France, assigned to 40 Squadron and flying Nieuport Scouts. At first, he was considered something of a boor by his comrades, helped along by a serious gaffe his first night in the mess, when he sat in a chair left empty by its former occupant, shot down that very day. Maybe his single-minded preoccupation with killing Germans set him apart at first as well. But that opinion began to change with his friendly, affable nature and the day he managed to pull his damaged fighter out of a "terminal" dive, an extraordinary feat of piloting.

He still had much to prove, for during the desperate fighting of April 1917, a time when his squadron took 50 percent casualties, Mannock's fighter was not even hit. He made no claims of enemy aircraft destroyed, either, and some of his squadron-mates began to wonder whether he was a coward. At one point the squadron log recorded that Mannock had spent forty hours on patrol without even a combat.

And then, on the very day on which revered ace Albert Ball was killed, Mannock got his first victory. A month later he shot down another German, and then he scored again and again, until by the end of the year, he had shot down twenty-three of the enemy. There was no longer any speculation about Mannnock being a coward; he was plainly anything but.

In spite of his poor vision in one eye, Mannock was a deadly shot. He practiced constantly and, like fellow ace Albert Ball, closed to point-blank range whenever he could. As he said after one victory: "I was only ten yards away from him . . . a beautifully colored insect he was—red, blue, green and yellow. I let him have 60 rounds, so there wasn't much left of him." By the end of 1917, he had been promoted to captain and won his first Military Cross, and with the rest of the squadron had traded in their Nieuports for the SE5a. It was a great day for the squadron in general and Mannock in particular, for the SE may well have been the war's deadliest fighter, rivaled only by the Sopwith Camel. It was tough, maneuverable, and at 135 miles per hour was one of the fastest birds on either side.

Mannock flew always with fear; he made no secret of it, and worked hard to control it. In particular, he feared burning to death, a phobia shared with many other pilots who flew the flimsy, highly flammable aircraft of the day. He took his revolver with him whenever he flew, "to finish myself off as soon as I see the first sign of flames," there being no parachutes in the fighters of the day.

His fear of fire did not impinge on the sheer brilliance of his flying, his aggressiveness, or the deadly accuracy of his shooting. As one of his citations put it,

> *he has driven off a large number of enemy machines, and has forced down three balloons . . . attacking the enemy at close range and low altitudes under heavy fire from the ground.*

His commander in 74 Squadron perfectly described Mannock the fighting man as "an extraordinarily good shot and a very good strategist;

he would place his flight team high against the sun and lead him into a favorable position where they would have the maximum advantage."

Then would come the hell fire charge to very close quarters, slowing to some degree in the last seconds to give everybody in his flight the opportunity to reach a first-class attitude from which to open fire. As a flight leader, he would not permit his pilots to go "swanning off" on a lone-hand expedition. When they attacked, Mannock insisted that they do so as a team. His commander called him "the most skillful patrol leader in World War I," high praise indeed. Another of his pilots added, "Flying with Mannock is perfectly safe. His leadership is foolproof."

He held back from making claims of downed aircraft unless he was absolutely sure he had made a kill, and increasingly he "mother-henned" green pilots through their introduction to war in the air. It was commonly believed that some of the kills credited to new pilots had in fact been Mannock's, assigned by Mannock to the new pilot's credit to boost his confidence.

He took very hard the death in action of any of his youngsters, and on at least one occasion could be heard sobbing deep in the watches of the night after a squadron-mate had been killed that day. And he was a trainer, too; one of his charges in 40 Squadron was a promising new pilot, Lt. George McElroy—Mannock called him "McIrish"—who would finish the war as the tenth-highest RFC ace, with forty-six victories.

Mannock was a formidable fighting-machine. During a single week of war, Mannock downed seven German aircraft, and during another five-day period, he destroyed eight more. His tactics were reminiscent of Albert Ball: attack, attack, attack, and shoot straight from very close range. Ever the good leader, he created a list of fifteen battle tactics intended to keep his men both safe and successful. They are simple maxims, but are a basic bible of air combat in World War I. They are worth repeating here:

1. Pilots must dive to attack . . . hold their fire until they get within one hundred yards of their target.

2. Achieve surprise by approaching from the east [the German side].

3. Utilize the sun's glare and clouds to achieve surprise.

4. Pilots must keep physically fit by exercise and the moderate use of stimulants.

5. Pilots must sight their guns and practice as much as possible, as targets are normally fleeting.

6. [E]very aeroplane is to be treated as an enemy until it is certain it is not.

7. Pilots must learn where the enemy's blind spots are.

8. Scouts must be attacked from above and two-seaters from beneath their tails.

9. Pilots must practice quick turns, as this maneuver is used more than any other in a fight.

10. Pilots must practice judging distances in the air, as these are very deceptive.

11. Decoys must be guarded against—a single enemy is often a decoy—therefore the air above should be searched before attacking.

12. If the day is sunny, machines should be turned with as little bank as possible, otherwise the sun glistening on the wings will give away their presence at a long range.

13. Pilots must keep turning in a dog fight and never fly straight except when firing.

14. Pilots must never, under any circumstances, dive away from an enemy, as he gives his opponent a non-deflection shot. Bullets are faster than aeroplanes.

15. Pilots must keep their eye on their watches during patrols, and on the direction and strength of the wind.

Mannock was described by the head of a family with which he lived for a while as "a socialist" and "deeply patriotic . . . a kinder, more thoughtful man you could never meet." He was a man of very broad interests who would "talk into the early hours of the morning if you let him" on about any subject under the sun. His patriotism, his love of England, was central to his life: He told fellow ace J. T. McCudden that England was the "best God damned country in the world . . . any man who wasn't ready to die for it had no right to call himself an Englishman."

Mannock finished his tour with 40 Squadron on the first day of 1918 and went back home on leave, looking forward to a rest from the war in the air. But he soon joined 74 Squadron— called the Tiger Squadron— then in its forming-up stage. He was back in France by the end of March, flying the tough SE5a and leading A Flight of the 74th. After the loss of one of his pilots, the squadron noticed that Mannock's loathing of the enemy had increased. His score continued to rise. By the end of June, it would reach fifty-nine.

His care for his men remained as it always had, almost fatherly. His approach to killing the enemy also remained: careful and professional but almost a crusade. One of his pilots described one of Mannock's victories as "a remarkable exhibition of cruel, calculated Hun-strafing," as he followed a disabled German fighter down, still firing on it as it fell to the ground. On at least one occasion, he strafed the crew of a crashed German aircraft, simply commenting "the swines are better off dead. No prisoners." And on a day when he downed four enemy aircraft, he trumpeted with obvious pleasure, "Flamerinoes, four! Sizzle, sizzle, wonk!"

His loathing of the German enemy never changed. The story goes that a British journalist doing a newspaper article on Mannock tore up his notes after interviewing Mick, exclaiming in horror, "The man is a monster. The Germans would be justified in considering us barbarians if they could hear him talk!" But then, the journalist hadn't been treated to time in a Turkish prison or seen friends fall in a flaming aircraft.

By the end of May, he had been twice awarded the Distinguished Service Order. Then, in June, came promotion to major, and the ultimate accolade: assignment as the new commander of 85 Squadron, replacing the brilliant Canadian ace Billy Bishop. By all accounts Mannock was a hard-driving, successful leader, but the inevitable price of the long days of hard service and danger was at last coming due.

Gone, said one good friend, was "the old sparkle we knew so well; gone was the incessant wit." Mannock's hands shook, though he wrung them to try to diminish and hide the shaking. When the shaking got impossible to control, he would leave the room. On one occasion, wrote this same friend,

we were sitting talking quietly when his eyes fell to the floor and he started to tremble violently. He cried uncontrollably. His face, when he lifted it, was a terrible sight. Later he told me that it had been a "bit of nerves," and that he felt better for a good cry. He was in no condition to return to France, but in those days such things were not taken into account.

He became convinced of his own impending death. Told by a friend, "they'll have the red carpet out for you after the war, Mick," Mannock said only, "There won't be any 'after the war' for me." As 1918 rolled on, he became more and more depressed, afraid that this, his third tour of duty, would be the unlucky one, but it did not affect his loathing of his German enemies, nor his vivid courage and leadership in action.

On July 26th, shortly after dawn, Mannock knocked down still another German, a two-seater. That victory would be his last.

He was flying with a green pilot, Lt. Donald Inglis, and after his victory led the lieutenant on one or two low-level passes over the wreckage of the German aircraft. As so often happened, the fight had been over German territory, and the two aircraft attracted a mass of gunfire from the Germans close below, including at least one machine gun.

The low-level pass with one of his men was most un-Mannock-like behavior, and maybe the best evidence of the deteriorated state of his nerves and judgment. And as they pulled away, Inglis saw flame on Mannock's engine cowling; then one of Mick's wings collapsed, and his SE turned for the ground, crashed, and burned. Maybe he was hit by ground fire; maybe the German two-seater gunner had gotten a round into the SE's engine; maybe it was simple mechanical failure. The cause of the crash really doesn't matter much, except that Mick Mannock was gone.

Inglis later crash-landed with a hole in his fuel tank, and as he was pulled from his wrecked fighter by friendly hands, he said to his rescuers, "They killed him. The bastards killed my major. They killed Mick." It was the finest possible testament to Mannock's leadership.

What happened to Mick Mannock after the crash is not clear, but he was probably buried by a German soldier. His grave was unmarked, but the German was a civilized man, who returned his enemy's identity disks and other personal effects to his family through the Red Cross. Lord Ashcroft, author of several fine books on war in the air, had possession of the disks, and writes that their "pristine state" suggests that they were not exposed to fire in that burning SE; it follows that Mick had either been thrown clear of the crash, jumped before his fighter hit the ground, or shot himself as he promised and fell lifeless from the aircraft. It's a reasonable, sound thesis, and every reader hopes he was spared the one thing he really feared.

So Maj. Mick Mannock was dead at only thirty-one, one of the most decorated warriors of all time. In just fifteen months, he had won the Victoria Cross, three awards of the Distinguished Service Medal, and two Military Crosses. Other less formal honors abound: A reserve RAF training squadron is named for him, as is a street in Wellingborough and an RAF VC-10. And the memorial an RFC officer would probably like best took place in 2014. At Wellingborough the Waendel Walk Beer Festival featured a Flyer Pale Ale, which, it said, "was brewed to commemorate Major Mick Mannock, VC, Wellingborough's own flying ace."

Though some sources claimed that Mannock matched Billy Bishop's score of seventy-two downed aircraft, his official score remains at sixty-one. It's a record that will long endure, but it is almost surely inaccurate, given Mannock's custom of giving credit to green British pilots in his squadron. Official policy permitted claiming as a personal victory a downed enemy aircraft shared with another pilot, but Mannock passed up that credit to add all possible weight to his new men's confidence.

Mick would probably be proudest of another legacy he left: young pilots who survived because he coached them and taught them how to stay alive and do their duty well.

There were lots of those.

CHAPTER FOUR

The Pride of Canada

Billy Barker (RFC Canadian)

He was the most heavily decorated military man in the history of Canada, which is saying a very great deal. He was a farm boy, with all the self-sufficiency and common sense that go with growing up in the country. He lived on his father's farm and helped work both the farm and the family sawmill; as he grew older, he became the appointed hunter for the sawmill hands, sometimes skipping school with his Winchester to make sure there was meat on the table.

When he was at school, he was a first-class student, but like so many other kids, he fell in love early with the wide sky above him, watching barnstorming pilots flying in country exhibitions. He was also a Boy Scout, and a member of a reserve cavalry unit . . . until war came in the autumn of 1914. He then enlisted in the 1st Canadian Mounted Rifles, and was in France by the next autumn as a machine-gunner. He remained in that job until he transferred to the RFC as an enlisted observer early in the spring of 1916; he was commissioned in April of that year.

Flying as an observer meant he was also the gunner, and Barker the country boy and expert shot got two kills of German fighters during the summer of 1916. He also received the Military Cross for spotting and bringing fire down on a large force of German troops massing to counterattack a Canadian unit. A second MC came the next spring for a similar action, along with credit for another German aircraft driven down. The summer of 1917 also brought a head wound from German ground fire, and a brief tour as an instructor in England.

By October he was back in France, flying his favorite airplane, the Sopwith Camel. He had several victories before his 28 Squadron was transferred to Italy, not long before Italy's crushing defeat at Caporetto, and the victory string got longer there. He took a steady toll of the Austrian and German opposition, and with other help rushed by the Allies, the Italians rallied along the Piave River to halt the enemy's advance.

Among his triumphs in the air was some balloon-busting. One notable flight occurred on a misty day along the Piave River with frequent Canadian wingman Lt. Steve Hudson. The two had said they were off to "test guns," and the guns indeed functioned very well indeed. The two jumped no fewer than five Drachen and got them all, without the usual danger of accurate ground fire, shrouded by the mist.

Barker was game for any aerial adventure, including spy insertion, which as usual he did his way. He had a trap door rigged in the base of the fuselage of whatever Italian bomber he flew for the occasion. The spy was packed into the airplane over the trap, and when Barker—not the spy—judged he was over the correct position, the spy went out, willy-nilly. Barker and a brother officer won an Italian medal for their courage in flying at night—probably at extremely low altitude—to drop a crate of homing pigeons to an Italian spy.

By mid-April of 1918, he was commanding 139 Squadron, equipped with the formidable Bristol Fighter . . . all except Barker, who kept his beloved Camel and continued to fly it. It served him well: It flew more than four hundred operational hours—out of Barker's grand total of more than nine hundred—and was his warhorse for forty-six victories over enemy aircraft and balloons. It had character, too. Barker didn't like the limitation to upward visibility created by the upper wing, and so he had "modified" that wing by cutting away pieces of the center section. He had also replaced the standard RAF gunsight with one he was used to from his boyhood, a rear-notch, front-bead sight, the kind he used to bring meat home to the sawmill.

In Italy Barker also laid the groundwork for part of one of Ernest Hemingway's famous short stories, "The Snows of Kilimanjaro," in which the dying hero reminisces over an exploit in World War I. Barker and a wingman strafed a German airfield, leaving behind them a flaming hangar, several damaged aircraft, and a dropped note, "Happy Christmas." Hemingway liked the exploit so much that it became part of his hero's last maunderings.

At last, in September of 1918, Barker was transferred to RAF Headquarters in London; he was to command the fighter-training aerodrome; but before he settled in, he used his recent absence from France as a basis to request his superiors to allow him ten days and a fighter to learn what was new there. He would do so, in spades.

This time he chose to fly the Sopwith Snipe, the two-gun next generation of his favorite Camel, a fast fighter that would fly with ease above twenty thousand feet. And in it he fought a monumental action, a storied, single-handed fight against long odds that won him the Victoria Cross. He had already flown the Snipe to three victories on his short trip to France, when, on October 17, he took off to return to England. On the way he attacked a Rumpler observation plane, which he shot down; but a Fokker had gotten behind him during his victory. Its fire chewed open his right leg, badly wounding him, but Barker turned on the German and shot him out of the sky in flames.

By now the sky seemed to be full of enemy aircraft, Fokker D VIIIs and Albatros fighters, and Barker was wounded again, this time in the other leg. But he got two more kills before he passed out and went into a spin. When he came to, he was still in the midst of a swarm of German fighters, but he bored into them, firing at one until it exploded. Somewhere around this time, he was wounded yet again, this time in the left elbow.

Barker now passed out again, but revived enough to struggle to reach the British lines and crash-land the crippled fighter. It turned over when it hit the ground, but men of a nearby Scots outfit pulled him out of the wreckage and he was taken to medical help by an RAF kite balloon unit. A Rouen hospital worked desperately to save Barker's life. He lay unconscious for two weeks and was finally evacuated to England in mid-January.

Barker's wounds were so disabling that not until March 1, 1919, was he able to make the short walk to receive his Victoria Cross in the brief ceremony at Buckingham Palace. That decoration, the equivalent of America's Congressional Medal of Honor, made him the most decorated Canadian soldier of the war. Besides the VC he held two awards of the Distinguished Service Order, three of the Military Cross, three Mentions in Despatches, the French *Croix de Guerre*, and two Italian Silver Medals for Valor. His only close rivals for the title of "most decorated" man in the British forces were fellow fighter pilots Mick Mannock and James McCudden.

Billy Barker survived the war as Mannock and so many other ace pilots did not, but he was never the same man physically; he had trouble with his legs after the war, and movement in his left arm was badly limited, but his spirit was as tough as ever. After the war, which he finished as a lieutenant-colonel, he became a business partner of fellow Canadian ace Billy Bishop. That lasted some three years, until he rejoined the new Royal Canadian Air Force (RCAF) as a wing commander, and for a time was its acting director. He has the distinction of introducing the use of parachutes and spent some time with the RAF in Iraq studying the modern use of airpower. He later became the first president of the Toronto Maple Leafs and president of Fairchild Aircraft in Montreal.

That career, seemingly successful, was also a continuation of the sacrifices he had already made for his country. There would be no recovering from his wounded legs, and he had only limited used of the battered elbow. It was probably those afflictions that led to the alcoholism that plagued his later days.

The brilliant career and the pain in his elbow and legs came to an end in March of 1930, while he was doing a demonstration flight for the RCAF near Ottawa. His Fairchild biplane trainer clobbered in, and Billy Barker was gone, far past suffering. He was still only thirty-five, and the fighting was long past . . . but even so he was a casualty of the War to End All Wars.

Canada realized the stature of the man she had lost. Barker's state funeral drew a saddened throng of military officers and government officials, six other VCs, an honor guard of two thousand Canadian troops, even a contingent of American soldiers sent to pay tribute to a great ally. It is estimated that some fifty thousand people lined Barker's route to the cemetery. He has all kinds of good things named for him, from schools to an airport to a squadron of the Royal Canadian Air Cadets. And the crowning touch came in 2011, when a memorial was set up at Mount Pleasant Cemetery, where he is interred. Its inscription speaks for Canada, and speaks volumes:

> *The most decorated war hero in the history of Canada,*
> *the British Empire, and the Commonwealth of Nations.*

CHAPTER FIVE

When the Royal Navy Ruled the Air

Raymond Collishaw (RN)

Son of a Welsh couple who immigrated to British Columbia, Ray Collishaw went to work young, as working-class kids did at the turn of the twentieth century. At fifteen he went to sea as a cabin boy, and after that learned the seaman's trade from the bottom up. By 1915 he was a first mate, and like so many other patriotic young men, he was eager to switch to the regular naval service.

When the Royal Navy was slow in processing his request to join, he opted for the Royal Naval Air Service, and after training as a pilot was sent to a place called Ochey, France, flying Sopwith one-and-a-half-strutters. He got his first victory in late 1916. He followed that with a double, a feat that earned him a French Croix de Guerre. Shortly thereafter came the first of a series of crashes, from which Collishaw made a habit of calmly walking away, unhurt and smiling.

His luck was legendary. He crashed or crash-landed several times and walked away, but he had his biggest stroke of luck on a day much later, when he landed in the fog at the wrong airport. Now landing at somebody else's aerodrome was not uncommon in bad weather or because of mechanical failure or battle damage, but you ordinarily didn't find planes with German insignia lined up on the tarmac as you taxied by. Collishaw forthwith roared off into the fog again as German troops poured out to arrest this interloper.

By the latter part of May 1917, Collishaw was a flight commander with No. 10 Naval Squadron. The five-man flight, all Canadians, had elected to call themselves "the All-Black Flight," and to paint their Sopwith triplanes a distinctive black. And each man chose a fitting name for the aircraft he flew. Collishaw elected to call his triplane *Black Maria* (then a slang synonym for a hearse); the other men took to the air in *Black Prince*, *Black Sheep*, *Black Death*, and *Black Roger*.

It was a happy gathering. In their first month as a unit, they claimed an extraordinary eighty-seven kills. The Germans that met them and survived quickly took notice of the Black Flight, and on June 6 the Flight outdid itself. Part of a larger group, the All-Blacks claimed eight German aircraft. Other aircraft of the Royal Naval Air Service got two more. Total friendly casualties were zero. Ten to nothing isn't a bad score in any contest.

In June, however, the All-Blacks lost one of their own, Gerry Nash, who fought a memorable battle with the two top German aces, Karl Allmenroeder and Manfred von Richthofen, the Red Baron himself, before being forced down with shot-up controls. He managed to set fire to his triplane, *Black Sheep*, before he was captured. It was a real blow to the remaining four All-Black pilots, who had to assume their friend was dead. And the next day, they ran into the von Richthofen *Jagdstaffel* and Collishaw fought it out with Allmenroeder, who finally crashed to his death. Nash found out that same afternoon, when a guard told him that Allmenroeder—then Germany's second-ranking ace—had been shot down by a black triplane. And high above the milling dogfight other pilots saw a "blood-red" Albatros flying, watching but not helping, the Red Baron apparently content to let men of his own service die without at least attempting to save them.

In January of 1918 Collishaw took command of No. 3 Naval Squadron, flying Sopwith Camels, and stayed in command—suddenly a major—when the Royal Naval Air Service merged with the RFC in April. By the end of that summer, he had been awarded the Distinguished Flying Cross (DFC) and a second Distinguished Service Order, to go with his first DSO and Croix de Guerre.

The Armistice was not war's end for Collishaw. Now a lieutenant-colonel, he was sent to Russia, his assignment to support General Denikin's White Russian troops against the Bolsheviks. After a hopeful start the White cause went steadily downhill, but before the ugly, brutal war was over, Collishaw had added another official aerial kill to his record and managed to sink a Red gunboat with a bomb dropped from his Camel. No statistics were kept in this little civil war, but it is probably fair to guess that Collishaw added to his score another twenty at least.

Collishaw stayed on in the RAF between the wars, serving in Persia and Mesopotamia, and when World War II erupted, he was sent to command an obsolete collection of aircraft called Egypt Group, based in North Africa. His motley group of Gloster Gladiator biplane fighters and tired single-engine Vickers Wellesley bombers gave the Italians fits, starting with an early airbase raid that destroyed eighteen Italian aircraft, carrying on with a strike that sank Italian cruiser *San Giorgio*.

The single modern Hurricane fighter Collishaw used on lone-hand raids persuaded the Italians they were up against many Hurricanes based in several fields; accordingly, the Italians spread their strength in modern fighters thinly across North Africa, and even established some "standing patrols" over their troop concentrations, a colossal waste of assets.

Collishaw left the desert in July 1942 for a post with Fighter Command and for a while commanded a Fleet Air Arm Fighter Group. He retired a year later and passed away in British Columbia in 1976.

Raymond Collishaw's "victory" record, like those of the other leading aces, is still a matter of some dispute. He has been unofficially credited with as many as eighty-one, which would make him the war's top ace, even ahead of von Richthofen. That number is qualified not only by the usual doubts and lack of confirmations, but by Collishaw's known habit of crediting a new, green pilot with a kill that was really Collishaw's. That assisted kill was followed by hearty congratulation and well-spoken compliments. Shades of Mick Mannock!

Great leaders often share great habits.

Chapter Six

Escadrille Americaine

FRANCE CELEBRATED THE FOURTH OF JULY, 1917, WITH A WELCOMING parade for her newest ally, the United States. And in a speech on behalf of General Pershing, the American Expeditionary Forces (AEF) commander, Capt. Charles Stanton—he spoke French but Pershing didn't—spoke a line that has lived on long past that Glorious Fourth, "Lafayette, we are here!"

His reference was to the Marquis de Lafayette, who as a nineteen-year-old officer traveled to the new world and joined the fledgling American army against Great Britain. He served with distinction and was wounded at the Brandywine. So Captain Stanton was acknowledging Lafayette's help and what many Americans believed was America's debt, and American troops were there in France to prove it. Some would fly in aircraft bearing American insignia . . . but some Yanks had already been flying for France since the spring of 1916, wearing horizon blue.

At first the venture into the air had been half-serious, half a lark. The American Squadron—*Escadrille Americaine*—was at first composed of just seven Yanks. They had French non-commissioned officer status and were commanded—sort of—by two French officers. There was much partying. As one writer smoothly put it, "extravagant and destructive sacking of the local inns" was a fairly regular pastime, but that did not detract from their determination to fly and fight for France.

When the smoke blew away, only three of the first seven were alive. Of the total of thirty-eight who served in the squadron, nine were killed in action, and two more shot up so badly that they were invalided out of the service. Others were seriously wounded but returned to fight again. At the beginning they had much to learn, but there was never anything wrong with their courage.

It was proved over the tortured earth around Verdun, to become the burial ground to hundreds of thousands of French and German troops. "They Shall Not Pass!" was the French war cry, and by the narrowest of margins, the hated *Boche* did not. The Americans were in the thick of the fighting overhead, and their casualties were enormous, given the comparative few they were.

Bill Thaw, one of the very early Americans to fight for France—he started in the Foreign Legion—crash-landed with a bullet-torn artery. In June Victor Chapman tangled with the great German ace Boelke and crash-landed with a head wound. He was flying again almost immediately with his head bandaged—maybe too soon—and one day at dusk he was bounced by five Fokker fighters, shot down, and killed.

Kiffin Rockwell, one of the Escadrille originals, kept on fighting, but his fighting spirit must have been affected by the group's high losses. Rockwell wrote to his brother that he was going to fly the next day with another original, Norman Prince, "and we'll do our best to kill one or two Germans for Victor."

That next day he was shot down and killed by a German fighter attacking out of the sun. Prince lasted only another week or so more; flying home in the evening close to the earth, he hit a high-tension line.

The Escadrille Americaine sported a typically American insignia on its Nieuport Scouts, what they called the Sioux Head, an Indian's head with open mouth and full feather headdress. The legendary courage of the American Indian seemed to have found its way into the hearts of the pilots. Almost two years before America got into the war, a handful of her best men were fighting for France.

Until February of 1918, when the Escadrille became the 103rd Aero Squadron of the new United States Air Service, and the extracurricular hijinks of the surviving pilots began to simmer down. Along the way the squadron ceased to be the Escadrille Americaine, influenced in part by American isolationists—supposedly influenced in turn by German urging—and became a sort of anonymous group ... except for the many who still used the old term or the equally appealing *Escadrille Lafayette*.

And less than three months later, one of the last charter members of the old squadron came to the end of the road. Raoul Lufbery, then commanding the American 94th Aero, went out when the engine of his SPAD fighter caught fire. His squadron watched in horror from the ground as Lufbery sideslipped to both sides, trying to extinguish the flames, even climbing out of the cockpit to handle the stick, but the fire grew larger.

That did not work either, and so the veteran Lufbery crawled back toward the tail of his fighter and simply let go, falling three thousand feet to die on the soil of the France he had long defended. Like Mick Mannock and so many other pilots, he had sworn he would never die in the flames of his aircraft.

Thus ended the meteoric career of a group of young men who took up arms to serve a foreign nation. Some may have done it for adventure, but with most of them, maybe all, at least part of their motivation came from the conviction that France and Britain were in the right, and men of conviction ought to take their chances and help.

CHAPTER SEVEN

Hometown Hero

Eddie Rickenbacker (US)

SHORTLY AFTER THE WAR ENDED IN NOVEMBER 1918, ALMOST EVERY-one in Columbus, Ohio, stood in awe at the train station to greet native son Edward Vernon Rickenbacker, the greatest American ace of the conflict. Within a few weeks he was feted by some three hundred thousand people in Los Angeles, toasted as the greatest aviator of the war by the New York elite, and praised in a lengthy telegram prepared for the occasion by the president of the United States.

Yet within eight years Eddie was flat broke, indebted to the tune of $3.4 million in modern money by the failure of Rickenbacker Motor Company. The next year he was nearly killed by a pencil pushed into his chest during a bizarre automobile accident. "You crawl out alone or you stay there," Eddie later remembered. And when he did, Carl Fisher, a nearsighted automotive visionary, manufacturer, and investor offered him a hand up.

Fisher owned a fledgling operation known then and now as the Indianapolis Motor Speedway. Fisher opened "the Indy" in February 1909 as a proving ground. By late 1927 "the brickyard," so named for its early racing surface, was so badly in need of repairs that Fisher considered giving up and handing Indy over to real estate developers.

Eddie bought the track and developed a golf course nearby, all with borrowed money, all at a good profit.

Soon, he brokered a sale of Bendix aviation to General Motors, using his finder's fee to pay off the debts from his Rickenbacker Motor Company bankruptcy. In November 1934, while serving as public relations manager for Eastern Airlines, he flew a DC-2 from New York to Miami and back again to great fanfare, setting the stage to become general manager and, four years later, the majority stockholder.

In May 1935 he offered the first shuttle flights ever between New York (Newark, New Jersey) and Washington, DC. And although he quarreled with the newly created Civil Aeronautics Board, he jealously promoted airport development nationwide.

Between September 1939 and December 1940, he transitioned from America First isolationist to full-blown interventionist, and told reporters he expected the country to be at war by the following summer.

Eddie was expecting an uneventful business trip to Atlanta on Wednesday, February 26, 1941. He boarded the Eastern Airline "Mexico Flyer" at the airport named for his friend Fiorello La Guardia, who had been commissioned to fly the very same day in 1917 as had Eddie.

But that evening near Atlanta, when Eddie felt the left wing brush a tree during the landing, he jumped up and ran for his life toward the rear of the plane, even as the pilot overcorrected, striking a large pine tree with the right wing.

Seconds later Eddie was wedged between the bulkhead and the gas tank in the darkness with a shard of metal that he could not see pointing directly at his left eye. "Does anyone have a match?" another injured passenger yelled. Eddie warned him that the entire plane was now soaked in gasoline. Moments later he tried to free himself. The next morning rescuers found Eddie nearly dead, the injured eye hanging on his cheek nearly severed.

Yet six months later, when he arrived back at La Guardia, he told reporters he then suffered from only a few aches and pains. When they asked him whether the United States should get into World War II, Eddie simply replied, "We are in it and have been for a year."

During those first few months after Pearl Harbor, he toured forty-one stateside airbases in thirty-two days, bolstering morale among airmen who would soon be on their way to dangerous assignments overseas.

The press described him as grim, powerful, and determined, prompting Secretary of War Henry L. Stimpson to send Eddie on a secret, highly sensitive assignment to confront an American god of war.

Although now headquartered in remote New Guinea, Douglas MacArthur was making trouble for the president. This wasn't the first time, but most recently his target was George C. Marshall, chairman of the Joint Chiefs of Staff. No one was better suited than Eddie to quiet MacArthur down.

The battleship *Oklahoma* was still listing with its bottom up, fully visible from the airfield at Pearl Harbor on the evening of October 20, 1942, when Eddie and his assigned assistant, Col. Hans Adamson, boarded a B-17 bomber specially fitted for the trip. Adamson had popularized dinosaurs to the American public while working at the Museum of Natural History in New York.

"I wonder why they are bringing this cripple on board the plane?" wondered flight engineer Johnny Barteck, the youngest man there: Eddie was stooped over, walking with a cane, looking much older than his fifty-two years. Barteck thought Eddie should be in a hospital, not traveling across the Pacific.

Their first flight, at about 10:30, was very short indeed. The landing gear locked in place during takeoff, putting everyone on board in danger. After an emergency landing, the crew carried their equipment to another plane in the darkness, followed by the passengers. They left Pearl Harbor at 1:30 in the morning.

Once aloft, Eddie spent some time in the cockpit drinking orange juice and coffee with the pilots as the sun rose over the Central Pacific. They began a routine descent to Canton Island at 9:30 only to discover that their intermediate destination had disappeared. Or so it seemed.

Capt. Bill Cherry, a drawling Texan wearing cowboy boots, now realized that tailwinds had been stronger than expected, pushing them beyond Canton. Worse yet, nobody noticed that the internal works of the delicate octant used to fix longitude and latitude had been severely damaged during the crash landing. The airbase at Canton Island couldn't give them a radio bearing because the equipment for doing so had just arrived but hadn't been unpacked. Palmyra Island to their north couldn't help either. Even as the radio operator sent SOS messages across the airwaves, the pilots began preparing for the first B-17 water landing in history. The copilot was almost cut in two as the plane plunged into eight-foot waves at ninety miles per hour.

Crippled though he was, Eddie helped a crew member push three emergency rafts out of the plane into the rolling waves before leading everyone onto the wing. Within six minutes eight men watched the B-17 sink, knowing they hadn't had time to retrieve food or water. All they had were four oranges, two fish hooks, and some string.

They would have been quite a sight if they hadn't been alone in the middle of the Central Pacific. Most had ditched their shoes and pants anticipating a swim to the rafts that most had avoided by scurrying onboard from the wing. Eddie was the best dressed, sporting an expensive blue summer suit and gray fedora. Whatever the reason, Eddie took over informal command of the survivors.

During the first week he split and portioned out the oranges. As the second week began, they began daydreaming out loud about a banquet at the Mark Hopkins Hotel, high on a San Francisco hill, just before blindness afflicted most of them.

Eddie saved them from starvation on day eight by snagging a sea swallow that landed on his fedora. Nothing went to waste. The intestines soon attracted a small mackerel and a sea bass. Better still, a rainstorm that evening brought fresh water.

And Eddie saved them all again by becoming a taskmaster offering kindness and verbal abuse in equal measure, whatever it took to keep the men's chins from sagging onto their chests. The single exception was young Alex Kaczmarczyk, who couldn't resist slurping some sea water in the darkness and later died in Eddie's arms.

A flying fish that soared into one of the rafts ended any thoughts of cannibalizing young Alex anyone might have had. Captain Cherry overruled Eddie and insisted that the three rafts split up to increase their chances of being seen, a decision that may have saved their lives.

Planes began to appear, oblivious to the men shouting at them far below. And finally, on November 13, 1942, they were spotted by a pair of seaplanes and ferried aboard PT boats.

"God Eddie, I'm glad to see you," MacArthur said when they met twenty-four days later at the Port Moresby airfield. Eddie later learned that the search had been abandoned until his wife, Adelaide, persuaded Gen. Henry H. "Hap" Arnold to resume it. MacArthur didn't blame Eddie for the warning from FDR that he carried and arranged for him to visit Guadalcanal before returning stateside.

The next year Eddie and copilot James C. Whittaker published separate accounts of the ordeal. And in 1945 Eddie published a memoir about his dangerous life and speculations about the hereafter, a book thousands of people found inspiring. Throughout the war years, he promoted industrial defense, appeared before Congress, and flew to the USSR on behalf of the president.

Eddie stepped down as Eastern CEO in October 1959, resigning his chairmanship four years later. He spent the rest of his life speaking on causes he believed in. His memoir was published in 1967, six years before his death in Zurich, Switzerland.

Eddie was born in Columbus, Ohio, on October 8, 1890, the third child of former starch-factory worker Elizabeth Basler Rickenbacher and her husband, William, an often-unemployed brewer. When Eddie was fourteen, his father was mortally wounded in a fight during his lunch hour while helping pour a cement sidewalk. The day after the funeral, Eddie quit school and began working at the Federal Glass Factory, but he soon talked his way into a job as an apprentice auto mechanic.

In the spring of 1906, he began working for the Oscar Lear Automobile Company, which soon thereafter began racing cars. Company partner Lee Frayer took him to New York City that year to serve as Frayer's riding mechanic responsible for monitoring gauges, tire pressure, and opponents approaching from behind. In those days, riding mechanics were not as well protected as race drivers and died three times as often in accidents.

Although the Frayer-Rickenbacher team didn't finish their first race as a team, Frayer soon became a father figure for Eddie.

He soon began driving in races himself, changed his name to Rickenbacker, and gave himself the middle name Vernon in July 1915 to affirm his American origins in an era when German Americans were not always welcomed. And yet, one sponsor promoted him as "Baron Rickenbacker," a young Prussian nobleman who absconded from the Vienna Military Institute in a stolen Mercedes. Along the way he worked for or with William K. Vanderbilt, Fred and Augie Duesenberg, Barney Oldfield, pioneer filmmaker Mack Sennett, and other luminaries of the early auto-racing world. He never set a land speed record, as some biographers have claimed, but he did drive five races at the Indianapolis Motor Speedway.

Eddie became nationally famous by winning seven major races, finishing second twice and third five times before ending his racing career in Los Angeles, November 30, 1916; that month aviation stole his heart in Riverside.

He saw a plane on the ground in a field, and introduced himself to pioneer flyer and designer Glenn Martin. His first flight that day with Martin made Eddie dizzy, but his mind was made up.

About a month after that first plane ride, Eddie was on a ship bound for Liverpool, England. He'd been invited to visit the Sunbeam Motor Works in Wolverhampton, but there was a problem. Britain went to war in August 1914, and "Baron Rickenbacker" had captured the attention of British intelligence agents. He was detained, searched, and mortified by having lemon juice rubbed into his body, to detect invisible ink messages. Ten days later the agents released him.

On the return cruise to New York, he had an idea. Eddie told reporters that if the United States ever became involved in the war, he would recruit fifty drivers and mechanics to join an American flying corps. Five of America's top drivers volunteered immediately.

When Congress declared war on Germany April 6, 1917, Eddie raced to Washington, but the Army turned him down. Two months later he joined the American Expeditionary Force sailing from New York to Europe—but as a driver.

There is no official documentation establishing that Eddie chauffeured Gen. John J. Pershing on tours of the front in France, although American newspapers reported that he did. He definitely drove Maj. T. F. Dodd, second-in-command to Col. Billy Mitchell, founder of the American Air Service.

While so serving, Eddie witnessed German bombardments of Nancy from Point-Saint-Vincent nearby. On the return trip Eddie fixed an engine problem on Mitchell's personal vehicle and soon became his driver. By August, Eddie persuaded Mitchell that he should be sent to flight school.

Shortly thereafter someone, maybe even Mitchell, changed the age in Eddie's military records from twenty-seven to twenty-five, just young enough to qualify for preliminary flight training at Tours. From there he was off to Issoudon, some one hundred miles south of Paris, there to become chief engineer, a ground job. The airbase there was sheer chaos, a rock-filled mud hole lined by crates, gasoline barrels, and even bathtubs awaiting construction of living quarters. Quentin Roosevelt, son of a past president, and Hamilton Coolidge, son of future president Calvin Coolidge, were among the pilots stationed there.

The French Nieuport 23 planes then flown out of Issoudon reminded Hamilton Coolidge of toys. Although not officially assigned, Eddie took a Nieuport out for practice, demonstrated a controlled tail spin in late December, and graduated from advanced flight school the next month. On March 6, 1918, he joined fourteen other pilots ferrying unarmed planes from Paris to Villeneuve-les-Vertus (Villeneuve); plagued by mechanical problems, only six reached their destination. Yet the Americans had no alternative to the Nieuports, which the French had abandoned for the sturdier SPAD XIII. Worse still, the Nieuports had dangerous wing and engine design problems that sometimes cost pilots their lives.

Eddie and the other pilots stationed at Villeneuve became part of the 94th Aero Pursuit Squadron of the 1st Pursuit Group, just in time for a German offensive that was nearly successful. The 94th flew its first hostile mission on March 28 without incident, but Maj. Raoul Lufbery embarrassed Rickenbacker and Eddie's fellow rookie, Douglas Campbell, by pointing out that they failed to notice several other airplanes, including a pair of enemy biplanes flying beneath them.

April 12 found Eddie painting the new and eventually emblematic hat in the insignia of the 94th on the fuselage of his plane.

The next day two of his comrades scored the first American kills of the war. Eddie's turn came two weeks later on April 27, when he helped his flight leader force a German Pfalz D-III into the ground. Ten days later Eddie and another flyer engaged four German fighters. Eddie attacked from above, knocking down his prey, as had James N. Hall, who didn't return. Soon, the Germans sent word that Hall was injured and captured. Eddie replaced Hall as flight leader.

During a May 17 patrol, Eddie shot down a German Albatros, just before noticing two others closing in behind him. He ripped the leading edge of his upper right wing trying to gain altitude, then went into a ten-thousand-foot freefall; according to his own account, he only regained control two hundred feet above certain death.

Eddie scored a third kill five days later and a fourth on May 28, bringing him into competition with Douglas Campbell to become the first American "ace." This expression for pilots with five kills is of uncertain origin, but was adopted by the Allies as early as 1915.

Two mornings later he was in the air again, even though he had not been assigned to fly that day. He rose to fifteen thousand feet just in time to see some German fighters begin an attack on British and American fighters returning from a mission. One of the Germans would not fly again, and "Baron Rickenbacker" nearly ran out of fuel returning from a June 5 mission. He spent ten days in Paris recovering from exhaustion, only to be hospitalized for the same problem twenty-one days later even as his unit was relocated to Touquin in the Chateau Thierry sector, the very center of the battlefront.

Eddie was back in the air on July 10, now flying a SPAD XVIII he commandeered at Orly. His first SPAD flight caused him such ear pain that he was sent to a Paris hospital. Three days later his friend Quentin Roosevelt was killed in air combat. And while grounded yet again, Eddie dreamed that his friend Walter Smythe was killed in a mid-air collision. And so it was no surprise when an orderly appeared to announce that it was so.

The Allied leadership refused to permit pilots to wear parachutes, the "chair-borne rangers" in leadership positions opining that the easy availability of 'chutes would encourage pilots to abandon their planes at the slightest hint of trouble. Eddie considered this to be criminal negligence.

Eddie was back at the front on September 6, waiting for the stormy weather to break, even as the Allies planned the great assault that would begin six days later. He was in the air that day, strafing German troops retreating on the highway to Vignuelles, a major Allied objective. Eight days later, in the air above Metz, Eddie spotted and shadowed four Fokker fighters closing in on some American bombers. He picked one off only to realize that he was tangling with Baron Richthofen's fabled squadron. Within seconds he was fighting for his life with the group leader on his tail, but escaped. His seventh kill came the next day, succeeding Endicott Putnam as the greatest "ace of aces" then living, Putnam being mortally wounded several days before near Toul.

Even then, Frank Luke of the 27th Aero Squadron, whom we shall meet in chapter 9, began to emerge as the new competition within the 1st Pursuit Group, shooting down two balloons at dusk on September 18, prompting a bacchanalia the next evening.

Five days later Eddie was picked to command the 94th Aero Squadron, despite his lack of stateside flight training, because his colleagues trusted his strategic decisions as much as his skills in the air. Billy Mitchell himself complimented his judgment, fighting élan, and dexterity fifty years later. He went aloft that very day, promptly found a quintet of Fokkers, and attacked "with the sun on his shoulder," downing two Germans with hundred-round bursts.

Two days later, on September 26, the 1st Pursuit Group was ordered into the air several hours before dawn to support American and French troops attacking around Montfaucon; it was their first night mission. Eddie destroyed at least three enemy balloons that morning before playing chicken head-to-head with a Fokker. He ended that duel by doing a half-roll followed by a half-loop, positioning his fighter for his tenth kill before limping in to a small Allied airfield.

As the Allied armies struggled to break through the Hindenburg line, Billy Mitchell gave them a special mission in early October, sending thirty planes to destroy three strategically located observation balloons. Eddie picked Ham Coolidge as the lead balloon-strafer. He deftly dodged one of the manned balloons. Then, after destroying the first, he shot down an attacking Fokker before escaping to Allied lines. Several days later they were in the air again with refined tactics, twenty-four planes spread across a three-mile front, hunting observation balloons with Eddie commanding. He downed one Fokker in a dogfight, then one more, in the process rescuing fellow pilot Jimmy Meissner, but at a cost. Eddie's friend Wilbert White saved another pilot by intentionally colliding with an attacking Fokker. Badly shaken by the loss, Eddie sojourned in Paris for three days. By October 23 he was back behind the German lines, fighting four Fokkers, two of which he shot down before he returned home. And four days after that, Eddie took out another, just before Ham Coolidge was killed by anti-aircraft fire. Victories twenty-five and twenty-six (by most accounts) came on October 30. Word came on the evening of November 10 that the war would end the next day. In a last act of defiance, Eddie flew over the lines, firing the last of his ammunition toward the enemy, minutes before the Armistice.

Chapter Eight

No Engine, No Wings, No Bloody Hope

THE WAR BALLOON HAD ITS HEYDAY IN THE SO-CALLED WAR TO END All Wars, World War I. That long, bloody conflict saw vast advances in the efficiency of killing, among them tanks, aircraft, the submarine, the machine gun, and the flame thrower. However, even the aircraft could not entirely solve the commander's age-old problems. *What's going on over the hill? What's the enemy up to? How many are they?* And there was also the perpetual gunner's puzzle: *We can't see them. Are we hitting anything? Is our range too short? Too long? Wide right? Or left?* Both the artilleryman's questions and the commander's uncertainty could often be solved by an eye in the sky, some sort of platform from which a trained observer could call down range corrections so that friendly guns could more efficiently flatten whatever was in the way of the grunts out in front . . . or as the British often called them, the PBI, the "Poor Bloody Infantry." That steady platform could well be a wicker basket suspended below a kite balloon. Particularly at the start of the war, battlefield radio communication was in its infancy, including talk between air and ground. How much better would it be to perch in a balloon firmly tethered to the ground, look through a powerful set of binoculars, and call in the range corrections by telephone, over a line running down past your balloon cable and the winch below.

The balloon as an instrument of war was nothing new. It had its genesis back in the misty past, at least as early as the four centuries of the

Han Dynasty of China, starting about 200 BC, when paper balloons—the Kongming Lanterns—were used as signaling devices. Real military use of a balloon would have to wait for the late eighteenth century, and the French Montgolfier brothers. The lifting agent was simply hot air, although some people thought the smoke from the fires that produced the heat was the magic that made the bag rise.

Around 1854 Frenchman Eugene Godard developed a useful military balloon that was used against the Austrians in 1859 and again against Prussia in the disastrous 1870 war. But it was in the United States that the greatest progress toward military ballooning was made, with both Union and Confederate armies adopting this new means of observation, even directing artillery fire through flag signals. And Professor Thadeus Lowe, the Union's balloon ace, even used a balloon anchored on a barge for some firsthand observation on the Potomac, thus creating the world's first aircraft carrier. The Confederacy managed a few balloons, and even had its own balloon aircraft carrier, but the South's effort was hampered, and finally died, for lack of materiel.

A pair of enterprising Americans, the Allen brothers, brought the blessings of air war to Brazil, as their country's contribution to the devastating Paraguayan War of 1864–1867, fought between Paraguay on one side and the Brazilian "Empire," Argentina, and Uruguay on the other. Britain also tried out balloons for reconnaissance and artillery observation in colonial fights in the Sudan and Bechuanaland and again in the Boer War at the turn of the century.

Man had been experimenting with other ways to get up into the sky and stretch his field of vision. The US Army, among others, tried out a system involving an observer clinging to a sort of swing suspended beneath one or more monstrous kites. The device has a permanent place in the annals of the weird and dangerous, and found no place in the US military inventory. It is not recorded whether anybody used this peculiar system in combat; it seems to have been consigned to the Rube Goldberg trash can before the shooting started.

The observation balloon's heyday was over by the time of World War II, but barrage balloons were widely used as an obstacle to hostile aircraft, both on land and sea. Nobody who remembers those years can forget the skies of London filled with a vast flock of barrage balloons, or balloons above ships of an Allied invasion fleet. Nobody from America's West Coast can forget the threat of Japanese fire bombs—*u-go*—floated across the Pacific on little balloons. Some three hundred of them made it to the United States, resulting in fires and at least six deaths.

Which left World War I as the scene for the military balloon's glory days.

By the onset of World War I, inflation of a balloon by heat from a wood fire was ancient history. Now the lift was supplied by hydrogen generators, since helium was very scarce. The generators inflated the bag much more quickly than the heat from a wood fire did; the hydrogen lasted longer, too, although the stuff was very inflammable indeed; a balloon peppered with incendiary bullets was likely to become a funeral pyre for the man or men in the basket beneath it, for often the winch on the ground took too long to pull the balloon and its passengers to safety. Even if they could take to their parachutes, the blazing mass would sometimes fall faster than the men in the 'chutes, incinerating them on the way to earth.

But at least they did have parachutes, secured to the side of their observation basket. They wore a primitive harness and simply stepped over the side of the basket and let gravity pull out the parachute and open it. Which it did . . . mostly, at least. It might save them from a ghastly death, however. It was almost certain to help if their line to the ground parted in a sudden wind and they started blowing out of control toward hostile lines.

The advantages of balloon observation were obvious to most of the warring nations. Especially over the Western Front, over a land mostly without substantial high ground, it was a great advantage to have an observation point four or five thousand feet above and behind your lines from which to look down the enemy's neck and bring down wrath from above upon him. The number of balloon units rapidly increased in the forces of both sides. Many of the belligerents' armies already had balloon units in the summer of 1914, some shaped in the old-fashioned globe, some of them by this time built in the sausage-shaped configuration that would in time be standard in most armies.

In Germany the sausages were ominously called, officially and journalistically, *Drachen*, Dragons. German soldiers coined another name for them, as soldiers will; noting their resemblance to a prominent part of the male anatomy, they called the huge balloons *Das Maedschen's Traum*, "the maiden's dream." There were other undignified nicknames, too. Their resemblance to sausages was obvious, but in the German army they were also known as *Nuelle*—testicles.

Balloons were not highly regarded when war began, but their usefulness rapidly brought understanding and expansion. German units in the west, for example, began the war with just nine balloon units with two balloons apiece. Once the line units saw their utility, they swiftly multiplied, until by the time of the bloodbath on the Somme in the latter half of 1916, the Germans were able to deploy fifty balloons. By the summer of 1918, they fielded almost four hundred.

Attacking a "sausage" was a dangerous business at any time, since they were regularly defended by clusters of anti-aircraft weapons, and dangled wires to snag a passing aircraft. If they were surrounded by unmanned balloons, those also dangled cables beneath them. Some experiments were made with a machine gun mounted on the observer's basket, and as the war progressed, more and more observers communicated by radio. During the course of the war, the Allies shot down at least 240 German observation balloons. America's champion balloon-buster was tough Lt. Frank Luke, who has his own chapter in this book. The champion balloon-buster among all the Allies was Belgian pilot Willy Coppens, with a grand total of thirty-five.

Defending your side's balloons was imperative if they were to survive from dawn to sunset. That meant not only concentrating anti-aircraft measures around the balloon, but sometimes surrounding them with other unmanned balloons to serve as obstacles to attacking aircraft, even, says one source, to sending up balloons loaded only with explosives, fired from the ground if the attacker came close enough. Friendly planes helped out when they could, but no belligerent could afford to routinely commit standing patrols of fighter aircraft to static balloon protection everywhere and all the time.

Early in 1916 the rocket made its debut. Developed by a Frenchman named LePrieur, it could be mounted in batteries on the wing struts of a biplane fighter and fired electrically by the pilot. The rockets were not very accurate unless the pilots could close to short range, but LePrieur's invention had some success. Ordinary machine gun bullets tended to tear through the gas bag without doing great damage, unless one of them also put a hole in the observer, but that changed with the appearance in 1917 of incendiary bullets, which touched off the highly inflammable nitrogen. After that, in every army, only brave men chose to go ballooning.

A great many of them failed to return.

CHAPTER NINE

Burning Balloons Ahead

Frank Luke (US)

MOST OF HIS FLIGHT HAD RETURNED TO BASE WITH ENGINE TROUBLE when Frank Luke battled four German planes that were chasing his boss, Maj. Harold Hartney, on August 16, 1918. He came out of the sun and downed a flyer too slow or inexperienced to escape, or so Frank said back at the airfield after gunning his engine to attract attention. Hartney was the only pilot in the 27th Aero Squadron who believed Frank. Since he had arrived the previous month, the rest of the pilots had dismissed most such claims. The kill was never confirmed; from that day Luke took official confirmation forms on every mission.

Frank's grandfather Lorenz Luecke had arrived in the United States from Prussia in 1862; he enlisted in the Union army but never saw combat. Frank's father and namesake moved west with an uncle, eventually settled in Phoenix, made a substantial fortune selling water rights, went into silver mining, and eventually became involved in politics. Frank Jr. became an avid hunter, marksman, and football player.

April 1917 found him following an older brother into the Army Air Service. Frank applied on August 2 and reported for duty in Austin, Texas, late that September. He completed ground school, and then went to Rockwell Field in San Diego for flight school on the Curtiss JN-4 "Jenny." The hands-on pilot training taught the basics in small pieces. The students learned to take off, land, and, finally, turn their planes.

While there, he met Marie Rapson; soon they were engaged, but long before they had hoped, Frank was on the *Leviathan*, a confiscated German ocean liner being used as a troopship. In mid-March 1918, Frank and the rest of the 27th Squadron were ordered to report for advanced air combat training at Issoudin, which Gen. John J. Pershing considered "the worst mud hole in France."

The pilots advanced through eight different fields covering combat techniques, spiraling, aerial acrobatics, formation, navigation, and cross-country flying. Unlucky trainee pilots Pat Ingersoll and James Marquandt found a permanent home under the grass at "Field Thirteen," complete with white marker, but the rest finished training on May 1. Frank learned some rudimentary French before they left.

They soon began ferrying planes repaired at Orly to American Air Service airfields, but were soon pressed into service near Saints, where Maj. Harold Hartney, their commanding officer, reminded them that they would have to earn their standing with the more experienced flyers of the 1st Pursuit Group, which they were joining.

Frank made few friends himself in those early days, boasting of how he was going to knock lots of Germans out of the sky. And in time he did just that. But he broke the rules practically from the beginning. While on a routine August 1 reconnaissance mission, he broke away from the rest of the formation as it entered a cloud bank. That morning the 27th lost six pilots.

During an automobile trip with Major Hartney to check on a downed aircraft, Luke shared his hope of becoming a great pilot, swearing that the Germans would never catch him diving away from a fight. While in Saints, Frank always pitched his Saturday night craps winnings into the collection plate at Sunday mass.

But on missions he increasingly operated as a lone wolf, regularly dropping out of formation to hunt on his own; more often than not, he boasted that he got another Boche, sending an enemy down in flames. When called to account for these misadventures, Frank had ready excuses, claiming he was lost or had engine trouble. Some in his squadron interpreted this as cowardice.

Shortly after their Nieuport 28s were replaced by more powerful yet temperamental SPAD XIIIs, on August 16, 1918, Frank filed his first request for confirmation of a combat kill. Five days later Hartney became commander of the entire 1st Pursuit Group. Hartney's replacement leading the 27th was by-the-book Alfred Grant, who had little use for renegades like Frank.

But the Allied start of the St. Mihiel offensive gave Frank an opportunity to prove himself. Frank waited for orders with many others at the Knights of Columbus canteen in Saints, the evening of September 11. Fellow pilot Jerry Vasconells warned that their greatest challenge in the days to come would be downing observation balloons, which were protected both by ground artillery and enemy fighters. That challenge would lead Frank to glory and, all too soon, to his death.

These targets had little in common with Civil War vintage spherical balloons. Most were shaped like a sausage and equipped with telephones. An observer could sometimes ascend to five thousand feet, scout the area, then quickly be winched down, even as artillery provided defensive barrages. Most balloons were protected by four to six anti-aircraft cannons spewing deadly shrapnel at attacking pilots, plus an assortment of machine guns and even rifle fire if attackers flew low enough.

And there were other challenges. Few balloons could be destroyed in a single flight through the shrapnel. Worse still, once punctured by tracer bullets, the balloon turned into red flame and black billowing smoke, which often blocked the fighter pilot's visibility. Pilots trying to finesse the mission by coming in low were vulnerable to ground fire or entanglement in cables that could cut an airplane in half. Balloon-busting offered none of the allure offered by duels with German fighters. Many skilled pilots refused to engage balloons at all, leaving a perfect niche for lone wolf Frank Luke. He was one of the nine pilots from the 27th who took to the skies the morning of September 12; Frank was assigned to be the lead balloon-buster that day because he arrived late for the morning briefing.

After losing three German planes he chased into the clouds, Frank spotted a balloon floating just below storm clouds near Marienville. And on his third pass, he turned the Drachen into a ball of fire, and then began looking for someone to confirm the kill. He landed in a farm field where the American 5th Balloon Company was operating that morning, found two lieutenants who saw the whole thing, and had them fill out the kill confirmation forms he carried on every mission. No one would call him a liar this time. He spent the night there due to engine trouble.

Back at the base on September 13 near Rembercourt, a mechanic showed him that one of several bullets that missed him that day was only six inches from his seat. Frank went hunting the next morning with two other lieutenants who helped permanently retire a balloon near Moranville. He was back in the air that afternoon with his bunkmate Joe Wehner, another loner but a quiet one who never talked about missions.

Joe and Frank planned to separate from the other seven planes on patrol. Joe would stay at high altitude fending off German fighters, while Frank attacked the balloons. They assumed that the other seven pilots would provide reinforcements as needed. They found a target near Buzy, home of the German 14th Balloon Company; Frank turned the balloon into an orange ball of flame and had a second one in his sights, just before he spotted eight German Fokkers, two of which were coming for him. Joe turned and went right into the enemy formation, taking out the two closest ones, according to his own account, but later credited Frank with an assist on the second one.

Lt. Leo Dawson told the crowd that gathered around them back at the airfield that Frank was no coward, he was stark raving mad, describing how Frank dove for the Drachen twice despite overwhelming odds that he would be killed by ground fire. By then, the mechanics were filling Frank's bullet-riddled SPAD with petrol for an afternoon mission, just before Major Hartney told him to call it a day.

September 15 brought Frank a new SPAD as well as a new target balloon at Etain for the morning squadron patrol. Five planes turned back due to mechanical troubles, but Lieutenant Hoover pressed on with Frank, until they were spotted by German artillery and six Fokkers. In a separate action, Joe Wehner downed one and possibly two planes. And that afternoon during a second patrol, near Bois d'Hingry, Frank downed another balloon. When he returned to the airfield, his third plane in three days was too bullet-riddled to be flown, but Frank had a plan.

He proposed that the squadron strike the balloons at dusk, when artillery fire from the ground would be less effective. That said, such an attack would also be risky for the pilots, since neither their SPAD instruments nor their airfield would be lit. His commanding officer, Lt. Alfred Grant, led the mission, but Frank soon soared away alone. He flew toward the skies above Chaumont to attack yet another balloon in the descending darkness. His first two low-altitude attacks above Chaumont were ineffective, but the third set the Drachen on fire only about fifty feet above the German ground crew. Within minutes he landed in a French field, to spend the night and savor his fifth kill of the war.

While Frank was away, Gen. Billy Mitchell told 1st Pursuit Group boss Major Hartney to find a way to destroy more balloons. By the time Frank returned to Rembercourt at 1:45 the afternoon of September 16, plans for a "show flight" that evening had already been hatched. Hartney had arranged artillery barrages supporting more balloon attacks at dusk. While they waited to attack, Frank bragged to Eddie that two German balloons in the far distance would explode at 7:15 and 7:19. A few hours later, General Mitchell watched in amazement as the gloom lighted up twice, just about on the schedule that Frank had predicted, but not quite according to plan.

Frank and his wingman, Joe Wehner, took out the first, Joe took out the second himself, but Luke, now separated in the dogfights that followed, downed a third balloon before they returned to Rembercourt within minutes of each other, not knowing that this was the pinnacle of their military careers.

At four the following afternoon, Frank and Joe destroyed two Drachens while avoiding anti-aircraft fire. And when the barrage stopped abruptly, they knew that German Fokkers were coming. The *Jasta 15* squadron chasing them included Georg von Hantelmann, whose fuselage sported a death's head insignia he earned with fifteen confirmed kills, making him an ace three times over.

Frank took out the lead Fokker, and then came to the rescue of an American pilot fighting with the French by downing an armed observation plane. When he landed to examine the crash (and the dead crew), someone from the French infantry photographed him.

But minutes earlier Hantelmann had killed Frank's wingman, Joe Wehner, although Joe was considered only missing for several days. The following evening on September 19, Eddie Rickenbacker threw a squadron party honoring Frank, now the highest-scoring American ace alive. Frank went on leave to Paris the following morning for a well-deserved rest. While there, he wrote his mother, letting her know for the first time that he was at the front. She need not worry, Frank told her, since he knew how to take care of himself in danger. His fiancée in San Diego, Marie Rapson, became an instant local celebrity when someone told local newspapers about Frank's exploits, as Frank became a nationally known public figure, seemingly overnight.

When Frank returned September 24 to Rembercourt, the St. Mihiel offensive was largely over. But his commanding officers, Alfred Grant and Harold Hartney, had found a way to get the 27th closer to the action by occupying an abandoned airfield and hangar north of Verdun. The next day Ivan Roberts of New York became Frank's new wingman. On their first mission together, Frank and Ivan dropped candy and cigarettes to Allied infantrymen.

Frank went balloon-hunting by himself the next morning, refueled at another American field, and returned in time for a 5:45 patrol targeting balloons on the Meuse. During the mission Ivan was shot down as they fought for their lives; his fate was not known for some time.

At dawn on the morning of September 28, without any orders to do so, Frank took to the skies and blew up a Drachen near Bantheville and then went AWOL once again, spending the night at a French airfield, returning to Rembercourt the next morning anxious to fly. He left for the scheduled 5:56 p.m. balloon-strafing sixteen minutes early, dropping a metallic cylinder containing a mess on the American 7th Balloon Company.

But Frank didn't come back from the mission. Although the details remain unclear to this day, the most reliable versions of events indicate that Frank destroyed one balloon that dusk, then turned his attention to another balloon that he may have destroyed before being mortally wounded by machine gun fire. He landed his plane, which is on permanent display in Terminal 3 of the Phoenix Sky Harbor airport, and staggered toward a creek near Murvaux before collapsing, exactly one year to the day after he reported for military duty.

Frank Luke was a fighting-man literally to his last breath. On the black day in late September on which America lost him, he had already downed three German *Drachen*, when he took a bullet fired by a machine gun on the ground not far from his third kill. The slug entered his right shoulder, tore through his body, and ripped out his left side. The wound was very serious and must have caused him great pain, but it did not stop him from strafing some German troops on his way to land in a field close to a stream.

He managed to get out of his fighter and stagger toward the creek, obviously heading for the cover of the brush that bordered it two hundred meters from his airplane. German infantry were closing in on him by now, calling on him to surrender, but still he wouldn't quit. He hauled out his Colt .45 automatic and opened fire on the Germans, and their return fire killed him, just as the anti-aircraft bullet almost surely would have.

One version of what is sometimes called "Luke's Last Fight" tells that after the smoke blew away, Luke lay dead, and he and his empty Colt were surrounded by seven dead Germans. That story is somewhat dubious on its face and is widely doubted, but it is surely what the tough kid from Arizona would have done if his body had let him.

America's top ace, Eddie Rickenbacker, summed up Luke's meteoric career; he was obviously deeply impressed, not something easily done with a man like Rickenbacker:

> *He was the most daring aviator and greatest fighter pilot of the entire war. His life is one of the brightest glories of our Air Service. He . . . shot down fourteen enemy aircraft, including ten balloons, in eight days. No other ace, even the dreaded Richthofen, had ever come close to that.*

And the message he dropped? "Watch for burning balloons ahead."

CHAPTER TEN

A Canadian Original

Billy Bishop (RFC Canadian)

William Avery Bishop was a bold young man destined for a career in aviation, or at least that's what the omens from his youth would suggest. At fifteen, at home in Canada, he created his own aircraft, made of pieces of wooden crate and cardboard held together with string. He flew it too, from the roof of his three-story family home in Owen Sound. It was a short flight, largely straight down, but Bishop survived, to be dug out of the wreckage by his sister. The crash did not dampen his interest in flight.

Bishop spent some time at the Royal Military Academy in Ontario, but when war broke out he joined the Canadian army and was shipped to France as a subaltern in a mounted rifle outfit. The trenches did not suit Bishop, and as a couple of months went by, he watched the infant Royal Flying Corps with envy. The life of a pilot in the wild blue looked good to him, and he said so: "It's clean up there! I'll bet you don't get any mud or horse shit on you up there. If you die, at least it would be a clean death."

And so Bishop transferred to the RFC. He signed on as an observer, since at the time there were no openings in flight school. Among other skills, Bishop became expert with the airborne camera, and trained other observers in its use, besides flying reconnaissance missions in the lumbering RE7. Suffering a badly injured knee when his aircraft lost power during takeoff, he spent some time recuperating in England and Canada.

Back in England in September of 1916, he won his pilot's wings in November.

He was assigned for a time to night-fighter duties, chasing Zeppelin raiders through the night skies over London, but in March of 1917 he got a transfer to 60 Fighter Squadron in France. That did not begin as a rousing success either, for he crowned several beginner's mistakes by crashing his fighter on landing before the vigilant eye of a General Higgins, who ordered him back to flight school. His squadron commander got permission to keep Bishop "until a replacement arrived." The next day Bishop got his first kill, an Albatros D.III, and the personal congratulations of General Higgins.

One significant piece of luck Bishop had: In 60 Squadron he met Corp. Walter Bourne, who had been Albert Ball's mechanic. Bourne explained some of Ball's tactics to Bishop, and from this meeting, the story goes, Bishop acquired his intense interest in ammunition for the machine gun on his fighter. Each batch of ammunition Bishop personally examined, round by round; a stoppage in the middle of a fight could get a man killed very quickly.

Bishop was naturally an aggressive pilot and favored a head-on, hell-for-leather charge straight at an enemy airplane. It was a sort of chicken game, which Bishop liked to conclude with a burst into the nose of an enemy aircraft, a burst that would damage the engine or maybe kill the pilot.

In short order Bishop became a flight leader and by early April became an ace, in celebration of which his mechanic painted his Nieuport's nose; Albert Ball's fighter already had a red nose, so Bishop's mechanic chose a tasteful blue. The blue spinner was noticed on the German side of the lines. The aircraft of 60 Squadron won a formidable reputation with their German enemies, and Bishop was referred to by some German aviators as "hell's handmaiden." The finest accolade came from Ernst Udet, who called him "the greatest English scouting ace." Coming from a first-class pilot like Udet, that was the highest possible praise.

Among other legendary deeds, Bishop won the Distinguished Flying Cross for what a restrained citation called "signally valuable service," namely the destruction of "twenty-five enemy machines in twelve days"—five of which, the citation said, "he destroyed on the last day of his service at the front."

By temperament Bishop was the ideal aerial fighting-machine. To begin with, he had extraordinary eyesight, and was able to hit targets other pilots could hardly see. It also helped that he was absolutely fearless in the air; one story says after one mission, his mechanic counted 210 bullet holes in his fighter. That did not appear to bother Bishop, nor did the sight of an enemy aircraft plunging to its doom in flames, as that ugly sight affected so many pilots. Even the sight of his bullets tearing into a German observer did not cost this cool man any lost sleep.

Like Albert Ball, Bishop was fond of lone-hand missions deep behind German lines, and on one of these, in June 1917, he claimed three German aircraft leaving their field to attack him, and more destroyed on the ground. His claims on these single-handed missions would later raise questions, but if they raised questions with some of the other combat pilots, they were wonderful fodder for the morale of the folks back home.

His feat on this mission could of course not be confirmed, but it brought him the award of the Victoria Cross, said to be the only VC award for an unwitnessed action save the award to the Unknown Soldier. He had already received the Distinguished Service Order for fighting six enemy aircraft and downing two of them.

In the autumn of 1917, Bishop returned to Canada, where he married his longtime fiancée and was shipped off to the British War Mission in Washington, DC, to assist the formation of the fledgling American air force. He was back in England in April of 1918, now a major and commander of a newly formed squadron equipped with the formidable SE5. Once back in France he ran his official score to fifty-nine.

On at least one occasion, he and his pilot tangled with the *Jagdstaffel* of the famed "Red Baron," Manfred von Richthofen. One account says the Baron "moved out of the melee, setting up a duel" with Bishop. Bishop took him on, and even got a couple of rounds into the red Albatros before his gun jammed. The duel was aborted when the arrival of four Royal Navy Sopwith triplanes altered the odds and Richthofen and his pilots left the aerial battlefield to the British.

Enter now the Canadian government, worried that a man legitimately deemed a national hero might be killed. And so in June, as a matter of public morale, Bishop was ordered to return to England to organize the new Canadian Flying Corps. Bishop would rather have stayed where he was, and voiced his displeasure in a letter to his wife: "This is ever so annoying." But orders were orders, and on the morning of the day he was to report in England, he flew one last single-handed mission, which boosted his final claimed score by five: three shot down, and two more "forced to collide with each other."

His new post in England brought promotion to lieutenant-colonel and an enormous lengthy title, but it did not last long. The war was at last over in November, and Bishop returned to Canada. His total of seventy-two victory claims has been questioned by, among others, two official historians of the Royal Canadian Air Force, but the destruction and deliberate falsification of many German records and the wild confusion inherent in any dogfight make any solid resolution of that question impossible.

After the war he was involved in forming a passenger air service with William Barker, also a Canadian fighter ace. The business failed, and in 1921 Bishop and his family moved to England. There he became a chairman of British Air Lines, but the family fortunes were so badly depleted by the 1929 crash that they moved back to Canada. There he became vice president of an oil company, and in 1936 was appointed as the first Canadian air vice marshal. When war broke over Europe in the autumn of 1939, he was advanced to the rank of air marshal of the Royal Canadian Air Force.

He took charge of recruitment, and under his leadership some 167,000 men were trained; many more had to be turned away for lack of space in the training programs. This remarkable success badly wore down his health, and he resigned his position in 1944. He was fifty years old, and in that year his son commented that his father looked twenty years older than his actual age.

But Bishop remained active in civil aviation matters and volunteered to head up recruitment again on the outbreak of the Korean War. His health had gotten even worse, however, and this time the RCAF turned him down. It was just as well, for Billy Bishop died in his sleep September 11, 1956, at a winter residence in Palm Beach, Florida.

His service to king and country had brought him fame and royal recognition: Besides the VC he had won the Distinguished Flying Cross, the Military Cross, and two awards of the Distinguished Service Order. His name lives on in Billy Bishop City Airport in Toronto, in a great number of places and streets, and even in a musical, *Billy Bishop Goes to War*.

Bishop and his wife had two children, a boy and a girl, both of whom became pilots. Daughter Margaret Marise Willis-O'Connor, called Jackie, worked as a radio operator, and son William flew Spitfires in World War II. Both received their skills badges from their father.

There is likely to always be controversy over the accuracy and honesty of Bishop's victory claims. One veteran pilot stated the extreme view of Bishop's claims:

> *God Almighty! Excuse me while I vomit. This and other reports by the same pilot are the only ones in almost two years that have ever upset me, because all the RFC boys bend over backward in reporting.*

Today, whether and how much Bishop may have embroidered his victory claims is lost in the shifting mists of history. Maybe so, maybe not, and it really doesn't matter much anymore. For what stands out about him still is that he was a fine pilot, a superb marksman, and utterly fearless in combat. Add to that the wild action of an aerial battle, with every pilot desperately trying to attack the enemy and avoid getting killed himself, trying to look out for his friends, watching his fuel level and his location, and claims for enemy aircraft down proliferated on both sides. In the summer of 1940, for example, Germany destroyed the RAF several times over . . . and yet, the next day there were those pesky Spitfires and Hurricanes again.

What remains for Bishop is that he fought hard and well for his country, and when there was a need, he came back to do it again in World War II, when he could have stayed home. That's enough for any man.

Chapter Eleven

The Red Baron

Freiherr Manfred von Richthofen (Germany)

MANFRED VON RICHTHOFEN CAME OF OLD PRUSSIAN ARISTOCRATIC stock, born in 1892 near Breslau. He cannot technically be called "the" baron, for the noble title of "*Freiherr*" was held by all members of a Prussian noble family, which in this case included his brothers, Lothar and Bolko. Like others of that class, he was an avid hunter and horseman, and joined a *Uhlan*—cavalry—regiment in 1911. When war broke out in 1914, he saw service on both Western and Eastern Fronts. One of his first exploits was not encouraging, taking his bunched-up fourteen-man patrol into a French ambush and losing ten of them.

He got better at his trade with practice, driven in part by his overwhelming lust for martial glory. "I am trying hard," he wrote home, "to win the Iron Cross." But the time of the cavalry was ending, at least on the Western Front, and it was not long until the stultifying effect of trench warfare and the machine gun got most of the German cavalry dismounted. The heroic horseback charges of earlier days were no more. Von Richthofen was destined for supply duties, which did not please his Prussian heart at all. He is alleged to have sent this somewhat rash note to his commander:

> *My Dear Excellency: I have not gone to war in order to collect cheese and eggs, but for another purpose.*

Had he been mere *Soldat* Richthofen, that tone might have landed him in the guardhouse, but when he applied for transfer to the German air service, the transfer was approved, and in June of 1915 he became an observer-gunner. A meeting with famous pilot Oswald Boelcke led to pilot training. It did not begin happily; he crashed on his first training flight, but managed to get at least good enough to graduate to active duty as a bomber pilot. Another meeting with Boelcke led to a transfer to Boelcke's crack fighter squadron, where he finally got his first confirmed victory in September of 1916. Boelcke was killed the following month.

Although he did not lack courage, daring was not one of von Richthofen's attributes. He fought carefully, attacking whenever possible out of the sun from above. He was an excellent marksman, and he flew the Albatros D.III, a fine airplane. While flying an Albatros, in this case a D.II, he won a notable victory over RFC ace Maj. Lanoe Hawker, a Victoria Cross winner who flew the inferior pusher-engined DH.2. Hawker, who won his VC by downing three German fighters in a single combat, took a bullet in the head after a long fight, and von Richthofen's reputation was made.

Von Richthofen quickly set about adding to his reputation, shooting down twenty-two aircraft in three months. He was awarded Germany's coveted *Pour le Merite*—the "Blue Max"—in January 1916, following his sixteenth victory, the German measure for advancement to ace.

He was keeping careful count of his string of victories in the air. Most pilots did, but von Richthofen also commended himself on each win with a silver loving cup, suitably engraved with the date of the victory and the type of aircraft destroyed. He sent sixty of them home before the supply of silver dried up.

Also in January 1917 he took command of *Jasta 11* fighter squadron, and there he blossomed. The "red" part of the Red Baron legend got started when he had his aircraft—then an Albatros—painted red, and the members of his squadron began to paint parts of their aircraft red as well. The custom of garish paint, extending even to lavender and pink, would spread throughout the German air force (known back then as the *Luftstreitkräfte*). It was what the RFC's Mick Mannock meant when he described one of the German fighters he shot down as "a beautifully colored insect he was, red, blue, green, and yellow."

Von Richthofen's men had unparalleled success during "Bloody April" of 1917, when British aircraft flew close support over the ground offensive at Arras. RFC planes flew aggressively over the German lines in aircraft largely inferior to the Germans', and losses were very high. New British pilots often lasted only a matter of days, but the RFC kept at it, and close air support and artillery spotting for the infantry didn't stop. It was the height of the hunting season for Richthofen and his men; in Bloody April he claimed twenty-two kills, for a total of fifty-two.

About this time he rose to command a wing of four squadrons, the famous "Flying Circus," but even von Richthofen's luck would not last forever. For in July 1917 he and his men pounced on a smaller bunch of RFC F.E.2d fighters, a two-seat pusher aircraft that was, in the words of 2nd Lt. Albert Woodbridge, who flew in the fight, "cold meat and most of us knew it."

But the "Fee," as she was called, had a wicked sting of her own. Being a pusher, the gunner flew in the front seat, with a wide, clear field of fire. The pilot, behind him in the bathtub-shaped fuselage, could also shoot a fixed gun forward, and the gunner could fire to the rear from a third gun mounted on a sort of pillar firing above the top wing. To do so, how-ever, during the wild aerobatics of a dogfight, he had to stand up on the edges of his cockpit, facing his airplane's tail. This was, as Woodbridge put it—mildly—"a rather ticklish position in a moving plane two miles in the air."

Woodbridge told his tale to author Floyd Gibbons in the late 1920s, when Gibbons was writing his fine book *The Red Knight of Germany*. More of Woodbridge's story is worth quoting for the vivid flavor of what it was like to be a war bird in those far-off days. He relates the story of a fight against the Circus in vivid detail:

> *I fired my fore and aft guns until they were both hot. Cunnell [the pilot] handled the old F.E. for all she was worth, banking her . . . ducking dives from above and missing head-on collisions by bare*

margins of feet. . . . I saw my tracers go right into [four Germans.] . . . Some of them were on fire . . . nasty sight to see.

The encounter with Richthofen's all-red Albatros was head-on.

I kept a steady stream of lead pouring into the nose of [the Albatros]. He was firing also. I could see my tracers splashing along the barrels of his Spandaus [machine guns] and I knew the pilot was sitting right behind them. His lead came whistling past my head and ripping holes in the bathtub. We could hardly have been twenty yards apart when the Albatros pointed her nose down . . . and passed under us.

Woodbridge's fire had badly wounded von Richthofen, smashing into his skull, at first knocking him out, then rendering him semi-conscious and partially blind. He recovered enough to land in a field, but his injury left him facing repeated surgeries to remove splinters of bone from his head. He would suffer from headaches and nausea afterward as well, but to his credit he insisted on returning to combat, refusing to be moved to other duties.

German officialdom was naturally worried about the damage to civilian morale that would surely follow the death of their aerial icon. And it is true that von Richthofen seemed not to be quite the same man after his wounding and crash. But his return to action was successful . . . until the chilly day of April 21, 1918, the day after congratulations had poured in on his eightieth victory in the air.

On this day Richthofen's men ran into the Sopwith Camels of the RFC's 209 Squadron, which was covering two plodding Australian two-seaters spotting for the artillery.

The artillery spotters were no match for the German fighters in a dogfight, and 209's Camels rolled over and dived to help, in spite of being outnumbered almost three to one. One of the Camel pilots was flight leader Roy Brown. While von Richthofen was this day rested and healthy, Canadian Brown was a wreck. He was a veteran, with twelve kills to his credit, but his stomach and his nerves were shot; he had been "too long at the fair," as the saying went, and now he spent his time in bed between sorties, keeping his angry stomach at bay on a diet of milk and brandy.

Like all good leaders, Brown tried to keep a special eye on his new pilots, and he had told Australian Lieutenant May to take his best shot and then get out. Young May, in his first dogfight, had done just that, downed his German, and was headed for home as ordered, but before he could get clear, he had von Richthofen's red Fokker triplane on his tail. He could not shake him, and the two aircraft were down to two hundred feet or so while von Richthhofen methodically drilled bullets into May's Camel.

But Brown had seen his chick in trouble and was diving to the rescue, and von Richthofen, still shooting at May, did not see him coming. Brown opened fire with his twin guns, and bullets stitched up the side of the gaudy triplane, then crossed the cockpit; von Richthofen went down. The Fokker landed upright, then rolled into a shell hole some fifty yards from some Australian gunners and Lieutenant Mellersh, one of the Camel flight, who got his German and then made a forced landing below the battle.

Understandably, some of the Australians claimed *they* had killed the bloody baron, and no mistake, mate, for they had also fired at the triplane as it pursued May. But surgeons who later examined von Richthofen's body found his fatal chest wound could not have been sustained by ground fire, and so the end of the Red Baron belonged to the exhausted Brown. Later speculation, however, has settled on Australian ground fire as the probable cause of death, although at least three different soldiers have been nominated as firing the fatal round. We'll never know.

Gloom permeated the German airfields, and at the British airfield at Bertangles, von Richthofen's body lay "in state" until he was given a formal military funeral the afternoon after he died, with an Australian infantry honor guard and six RFC pilots as pallbearers. A chaplain in formal white surplice conducted the burial service, the ceremony was photographed, and a copy of the print was dropped over von Richthofen's home field.

Brown collapsed after the next day's patrol and for three weeks was delirious. He returned to fly again as an instructor in England, but passed out again months later and crashed. With several skull fractures, he was pronounced dead, but the doctors kept working, and he returned in time to full health.

Von Richthofen became an icon of the German war effort, what was left of it, as he had been in the war years when Germany still had some hope of victory; his stature only increased over time. It's a little sad that today a whole generation knows him only as the imaginary foe of the deathless, fearless Snoopy, wearing his helmet and goggles, still flying his aerial doghouse and shouting or maybe barking: *Curse you, Red Baron!*

CHAPTER TWELVE

A Brilliant Pilot

James McCudden (RFC)

IN THE US MILITARY McCUDDEN WOULD HAVE BEEN REFERRED TO AS a "Mustang," an officer up from the ranks. He had enlisted in 1910 as a Royal Engineer bugler, moving to the infant RFC about 1913 as a mechanic. In the early days of the war on the Western Front, he had begun to fly as an observer, and he was later sent back to England for formal flying instruction. Then it was back to France where he made the five kills required for "ace" status.

He was plenty good enough to earn a second return to England, this time as an instructor. He was a fine, careful teacher, but also a spectacular pilot when he wanted to be; he was, as one of his students described him, "a brilliant pilot, absolutely outstanding," capable of breathtaking stunts like this one, described by one of his pupils. McCudden would take off and immediately

> *loop directly off the ground when he was taking off and continue loop-ing! Once he looped thirteen times from take off and when he finished he was 500 feet high.*

But he was also the careful pilot, spending hours checking the mechanical condition of his plane and its weapons, and he coupled that care with phenomenal shooting ability. One of his colleagues called him a "shooting genius." Another pilot commented that

*we'd all go up and we'd fire at the target but McCudden would . . .
tear the target to shreds . . . he only had to fire a matter of 20 rounds
[at an aircraft] and the machine seemed to fall to pieces.*

McCudden returned to France, this time with 56 Squadron, now
as a flight commander. He was convinced that the war in the air would
be won by "beating the hun at his own game, which is cunning." He
preached caution to the men he led. "[A]lways attack the Hun at his
disadvantage if possible, and if I were attacked at my disadvantage I usually broke off the combat." Quite often this meant deliberately refusing
to accept the challenge, and cautiously retiring so as to get into a better
position. The only exception, he said, was when he saw friendly forces
"being overwhelmed by superior numbers of the enemy."

McCudden's leadership was, like that of all good commanders, concentrated on

*getting the job done with the least possible loss. He protected and
taught his young men carefully, and set an example for them otherwise. He drank very little alcohol and was careful to keep himself in
good physical condition, and he spent a lot of time on careful checking
of his aircraft and machine guns.*

McCudden the careful commander in fact preferred to operate alone,
much like some of the other leading aces like Albert Ball. He regularly
flew lone-hand patrols in addition to flight and squadron operations,
and at least one of these lonely flights produced three more victories in
a single mission.

McCudden's single-handed expeditions produced a serious casualty
rate among the German LVG and Rumpler observation aircraft, the vital
eyes of the German command. And when new models of these two-
seaters showed their ability to climb above twenty thousand feet, the
normal combat ceiling of the British fighters, McCudden solved that
problem by modifying his SE5a's engine until he could reach twenty-one
thousand feet. He was a scourge to the enemy high-flyers, and reached
the fifty-kill mark by mid-February of 1918.

Combat at those altitudes took a heavy physical toll on any pilot, and McCudden was no exception. At that height the bitter cold of an open cockpit coupled with the scarcity of oxygen robbed a man of his normal speed of thought and reaction; after all, Mount Everest's summit is only seven thousand feet higher. A comment by McCudden says a lot about both his condition and his determination:

What a beautiful day it was, but I felt so bad for my throat was very sore and the cold and height were affecting it.

Seven months of almost continuous combat was starting to take its toll on McCudden, and his commanders saw it. With fifty-seven victories, he was sent on leave, which included being much made-over in London Society and awarded the cherished Victoria Cross. His next step was to return to pilot instruction at Ayr, in Scotland, but McCudden was not content. He did his usual competent, careful job of teaching, but he soon began to agitate to return to the Western Front again, and kept up the pressure until bureaucracy surrendered. He was back in early July of 1918, now a major, and in command of 60 Squadron, a first-class outfit.

He flew in from England in a brand-new SE5a, landing at an airfield just five miles short of his destination to be sure of his direction. He landed the SE neatly, in spite of the difficult layout of the field, and, after confirming his way to 60 Squadron's airfield, took off again. His flight immediately went bad. Let a witness, another pilot, tell about it.

The aircraft took off into the wind and at about 100 feet did a vertical turn and flew back across the aerodrome by the side of the wood. The engine appeared to be running badly. The pilot rolled the machine which failed to straighten out.... It crashed nose down into the wood.

McCudden was still alive when rescuers reached him, but he was unconscious and he had a badly fractured skull. He died the same evening without regaining consciousness. He was only twenty-three.

CHAPTER THIRTEEN

Fierce Little Beast—The Sopwith Camel

THIS CHAPTER IS NOT CONCERNED WITH THE GALLANT SNOOPY AND his heavily armed flying doghouse, nor with a feller in a burnoose riding a dromedary across trackless sands somewhere west of Suez. It deals instead with some of the brave men of the Royal Flying Corps who flew the famous single-seat fighter so named.

The Sopwith Camel was an efficient killer . . . on both ends. It was a highly effective fighter aircraft—some say the finest fighter of the war— but it was also an unforgiving companion to pilots who were even a little careless. If you mistreated your Camel, it might very well turn on you and kill you, or break part of you, and it could do so very suddenly. It was said of the "fierce little beast" that those who flew her had a choice between "a wooden cross, a red cross, and a Victoria Cross."

For the Camel did not have a conventional motor, one in which the pistons went up and down in a solid block of iron or steel, driving a crankshaft. Instead, the Camel's motor was a rotary, that is, the cylinders of its motor were set in a circle around a drive shaft attached directly to the propeller. That meant that instead of prop and drive shaft revolving, the whole engine turned on its own axis, cylinders and all, imparting a ferocious torque to the flight of the aircraft, especially on takeoff. Its general effect was to cause the aircraft to climb in a left-hand turn and dive turning right.

The Camel was the lineal descendant of the Pup, also a product of the Sopwith Aviation Company, a small, handy fighter. Both airplanes shot down a great many of the enemy, but as one writer very accurately put it, while the Pup was "elegant and docile," the Camel was a "high strung animal." Its dangerous temperament was due not only to the rotary motor, but to the location of motor, cockpit, and twin Vickers machine guns, all within about seven feet of the fuselage of the Camel. The combination of the rotary engine and this concentration of weight made the balance of the little fighter very delicate, and was the reason so many pilots died or were badly injured in the Camel, particularly pilots just learning to fly her. In time the casualty rate in pilot training was so high that the RFC ordered a number of two-seat versions of the Camel.

The vicious torque was present always, but especially dangerous on takeoff, or in a dogfight close to the earth. It might turn the little plane into a spin, particularly dangerous at low altitude. It was a persistent danger, but it also saved some lives among those who flew her, for the Camel was magnificent in a dogfight; the only enemy aircraft that had a chance of turning with her was the Fokker triplane, but as an American ace commented, "not even the Fokker triplane could follow the Camel in a right-handed bank."

The Camel had a vicious bite, as well, for she was the first RFC fighter armed with twin machine guns. A fairing Shell rising to a curve around her guns gave rise to the nickname "Camel"—that was her hump—and of course she was fitted with "interrupter gear" to synchronize the guns and engine revolutions so she wouldn't shoot off her own prop. The Vickers guns were belt-fed, which eliminated the old problem of changing ammunition drums on a Lewis gun while in the middle of the wild aerobatics of a dogfight.

The Lewis gun—a pair of them—remained on those Camels assigned as night-fighters, for the simple reason that staring into the darkness over a pair of flaming guns destroyed the pilot's night vision. Two Lewis guns mounted on the upper wing took the muzzle flash out of the pilot's field of vision, and the Foster Mounts on which the Lewises rested allowed the guns to be pulled down within reach of the pilot when the time came to reload with new ammunition drums.

The Camel shone in the ground attack role and also as a day- and night-fighter. Ground attack had always been extremely dangerous for fighter pilots, with nothing but fabric and/or plywood between them and infantry rifles and machine guns at very close range. In time Sopwith developed the TF1 ("Trenchfighter") Camel, which provided the pilot some armor protection. Some TF Camels were even fitted with a rudimentary rack that would hold four twenty-pound bombs.

The Royal Navy got its share of Camels as well, modified so that one Vickers fired forward and one Lewis fired at a upward angle, handy for shooting up balloons and airships. A final touch added by the Navy was a dive-bomber role, by the addition of two forty-nine-pound bombs. In July 1918 seven Navy Camels flew off carrier HMS *Furious* to attack the German base at Tondern, in what is today Denmark. One pilot was forced to abort the mission, but the rest attacked, leaving three big hangars burning, with Zeppelins L54 and L60 burning inside them. A bonus for the RN pilots was a balloon and two hydrogen tanks. One Camel crashed, the pilot killed. Three landed safely. Three others landed in neutral Denmark, where two of the Camels were seized and one was burned by its pilot. All three of the pilots managed to escape.

The next month a Royal Navy Camel accounted for the last Zeppelin shot down during the war. Lt. Stuart Culley took off from what also passed for an aircraft carrier in those formative days, a flat-bottomed barge towed by destroyer HMS *Redoubt*. Culley climbed all the way to nineteen thousand feet and took on Zeppelin L53 off the coast of Holland. Using the two Lewis guns mounted on the upper wing, Culley downed the enormous airship, then made a water landing close to the lighter, which recovered both the pilot and his triumphant little Camel.

The Camel was an efficient killer. From its first service over the Western Front in July 1917, to the day of the Armistice, the Camel accounted for some thirteen hundred enemy aircraft; it was the highest number of aircraft destroyed during the war by any Allied aircraft type. It went on to peacetime duty with a number of foreign nations as well, including the US Navy.

Many of the RFC's finest pilots flew the little Camel. Von Richthofen's red triplane probably fell to Roy Brown's Camel—although there are also claims that Australian ground fire got him—and Billy Barker, Canada's third-ranking ace—behind Billy Bishop and Raymond Coll-ishaw—flew one to fifty-four victories in the air.

A teetotaling non-smoker, Donald Roderick MacLaren was also a careful pilot. The story goes that he not only spent much time inspecting his guns, ammunition, and interrupter gear, but carried only half the ammunition he might have—some six hundred rounds—to save weight. MacLaren and his Camel might have gone on to eclipse all the com-petition had he not broken a leg during a "friendly" wrestling match in October of 1918.

MacLaren, a fur trader before he joined the Canadian forces, went on to help organize the postwar Royal Canadian Air Force, and to a successful career in civil aviation, before his death at ninety-four. Among his memories were his two Military Crosses, the Distinguished Service Order, and Distinguished Flying Cross.

There were many other less well-known Camel aces, like Capt. Clive Collett, who downed eleven enemy planes including three in a single day. Wounded, he was assigned as a test pilot; flying a captured German fighter, he crashed and was killed.

Flight Sub-Lieutenant Hugh Maund, Royal Naval Air Service, flew the Camel to nine victories to add to an earlier two in other aircraft. Capt. George Hackwell, a Devon man, flying at night, shot down a Gotha heavy bomber in a Camel, and finished the war with the Military Cross and nine victories.

Another Camel ace boosted his score abruptly in a most unusual way. Already an ace with six victories, Lt. Howard Knotts was shot down by ground fire while strafing German road traffic. Taken prisoner, he was the very epitome of *never say die*, for he managed to set fire to seven new Fok-kers traveling on the same train on which he was. Understandably, the Germans were furious and there was talk of shooting him for "sabotage," but cooler heads prevailed and Knotts survived.

Ground attack took its toll on Camel pilots, as it did on others who flew those highly dangerous missions, and gave rise to British counter-measures. Besides the introduction of some minimal armor to protect the pilot, one squadron installed a 35-millimeter cannon on one of its fighters. This contraption was supposed to fire canister rounds—a canister of lead balls—but post-Armistice testing was a disappointment, since its maximum range turned out to be about 150 feet. It was quickly relegated to the dust heap of military curiosities.

At least two Camel pilots joined the exclusive club of those who had six victories in a single day. One of them, Capt. Henry Winslow Woolett, got his six on an April day in 1918, and finished with a score of thirty-five. The other, Capt. John Trollope, got his six the month before, then was shot down and passed into captivity with a score of eighteen but without his left hand, amputated after he was badly wounded.

American ace Elliott White Springs, often otherwise critical of planes and people, had this to say about the Camel: "they . . . could turn inside a stairwell . . . could make a monkey out of an SE or a Fokker at treetop level . . . in a dogfight down low nothing could get away from it." Another American ace agreed:

Although inherently unstable (rigged so tail-heavy that it would nose up and stall if flown hands-off), it was highly maneuverable, climbed well at low and medium altitudes, and, when properly handled, was a most effective weapon for close-in air combat at those altitudes.

It was all of that. For all her sometimes daunting reputation, the "fierce little beast" helped bring the biggest war of all time to a happy ending for the Allies. Camels flew and fought in many places besides the furious air war over France and the Low Countries. They appeared as fighting-machines in Greece, Italy, Turkey, Palestine, and other parts of Africa, and everywhere acquitted themselves well.

It's a pleasure to know that a few are still flying.

Three to Draw to

Airfighting in World War I was certainly the province of the eagles, those memorable fighter-pilots who became aces many times over, who achieved almost innumerable and undying fame even among people who knew little about that war or any war. The Wild Blue Yonder quickly became the stuff of legend, with very little known of the ugly side, the fear of catching fire in the air in particular, the fear that drove so many brave men to carry an automatic or revolver whenever they flew.

Not nearly enough credit was given to the rank and file of the fighter battles, the men who flew day in, day out, as the most famous aces did, who feared as they did, and shot down their four or eight or twelve or even more of the enemy. They carried the great weight of the battle high above the mud and dirt of the battlefield and did most of the dying. Without them the Great War would not have ended as it did.

So here are the stories of three decorated men who were all aces well known by their peers, but without most of the sincere but overblown publicity that marked the lives of the great high-scoring airfighters. These three represent all the hundreds who swallowed their fears and took their chances, and won in the clouds the greatest war ever fought by mankind.

Chapter Fourteen

Small Package, Deadly Contents

Andrew Beauchamp-Proctor (RFC)

Everybody has seen little kids peddling their tricycles madly up and down the sidewalk, their short-legged reach often helped out with blocks fixed to the tops of their pedals. Maybe the reader has helped a child out by installing blocks to help out short young legs. That can be a very good thing for the kids, but how about the same convenience for grown men in combat?

It worked very well for South African Andrew Beauchamp-Proctor, who stood just five feet two inches tall. RFC mechanics jacked up the seat of his airplane so he could see, and some wooden blocks were attached to the rudder bar so he could reach it. It sounds clumsy, and maybe it was, but it helped Beauchamp-Proctor to fifty-four victories in the air, making him South Africa's leading ace. Sixteen of his kills were observation balloons, which made him also the top balloon-buster in the British Empire.

He fought on the ground during the early days of the war, serving in the German South-West Africa campaign as a signalman in the Duke of Edinburgh's Own Rifles. He took a break after that, long enough to complete another year of his engineering degree from Cape Town University.

Then it was back to the service in the spring of 1917, this time as an RFC mechanic. He was soon commissioned, and sent to pilot training at Oxford, where he soloed after only five hours instruction, landing so hard that he destroyed his plane's landing gear. He was still graduated, for after all, his destructive landing came at the *end* of his solo flight.

His height and his inability to reach the plane's controls may well have caused—or at least contributed to—the wrecked landing gear. But he still was pronounced fit to fly and assigned to a fighter squadron, number 84, where he stood out among a galaxy of fine pilots. That squadron amassed a victory total of 323 enemy aircraft, and twenty-five of its officers would become aces. Some of this excellence was no doubt due to the squadron commander, Maj. William Sholto Douglas, who in World War II would rise to be head of RAF Fighter Command and an RAF air marshal.

For Beauchamp-Proctor the war began slowly. Never regarded as an excellent pilot, he was involved in no fewer than three landing accidents before he could ever claim a victory. His deadly aim made him a devastating opponent, however, even though his flying skills remained distinctly second-rate, and once he got started in the air, there was no stopping him. He would never rank among the flying-champion pilots, but he was a deadly shot, and on January 3, 1918, he claimed his first victory, a German aircraft sent down "out of control." And gradually, he began to concentrate on balloons and two-seater observation aircraft, although they were heavily defended, apparently with the intention of depriving the enemy of his eyes above the British lines.

In March he scored four more times. Three of these were the product of a wild five-minute battle on March 17. April was a fallow month, with only one victory, but by the end of May he had eleven for the month, and a total of twenty-one. In the first two weeks of June, his score rose by another six, including four more balloons.

He went back to England then, both to enjoy some well-deserved leave and to do his bit for the latest RAF recruiting drive. By the 8th of August, he was back in the air again, leading 84 Squadron, in company with American "Yank" Boudwin, taller than Beauchamp-Proctor by all of two inches, and six-foot-four Hugh Saunders. And on the 22nd he put on a daring, memorable show, attacking a line of six balloons, destroying one and forcing down the other five, while their observers intelligently bailed out.

In September he was held to four balloons, but in the first days of October he downed another three *Drachen* and three of Germany's best new aircraft, the Fokker DVIIs. On the 8th of October, however, he was wounded in the arm by ground fire and pulled off flying over the front.

Hospitalized until March 1919, he went on a four-month lecture tour of the United States. Back in England, he received a permanent RAF commission and qualified as, of all things, a seaplane pilot. In November of 1919 he traveled to Buckingham Palace to receive his country's highest honor, the Victoria Cross, to add to his Military Cross, Distinguished Flying Cross, and Distinguished Service Order.

The VC citation made mention of his excellence at a duty every pilot dreaded, with good reason: ground attack, with its attendant danger from massed machine gun and rifle fire from the ground at almost point-blank range. His conduct, said the citation, was "almost unsurpassed in its brilliancy."

Beauchamp-Proctor stayed on in the Royal Air Force, but in June of 1921 he unaccountably and suddenly came to the end of a brilliant career in the air. He was flying a Sopwith Snipe in rehearsal for an air show to be held at RAF Hendon. Nobody knows precisely what happened, but his little fighter went into a violent spin as he came out of a slow loop and crashed.

Beauchamp-Proctor did not survive. Some have speculated that his diminutive size may have contributed to the accident, but there is no way of knowing. His body was returned to South Africa, where, quite fittingly, he was given a state funeral.

CHAPTER FIFTEEN

Too Young to Vote

George Edwin Thomson (RFC)

HE WAS AN ACE SEVERAL TIMES OVER, A MASTER OF THE UNFORGIVING Sopwith Camel, a well-known athlete, and a captain in the Royal Flying Corps . . . all before his twenty-first birthday; and that birthday had not been reached at the time of his death.

George Edwin Thomson was born of British parents in Burma, but educated in Scotland in the last halcyon days of peace, his eyes on a civil service career. He was well known as an athlete, both as a swimmer and a rugby player. But World War I put his dreams on hold, as it did so many others, and instead of entering the civil service, he became an officer in the King's Own Scottish Borderers.

He was moved to the Royal Flying Corps as a second lieutenant in the autumn of 1916 for pilot training, which he successfully completed in spite of a crash that left his face permanently scarred. It would not be his only mishap. One curious event happened in France when his new squadron was moving from one airfield to another. At a stop at St. Omer along the way, Thomson miscalculated what should have been a routine landing and undershot, settling down on top of a Bessonneau Hangar, a contraption with a canvas roof. One of Arthur Gould Lee's excellent books on airfighting in World War I describes it neatly:

> *Thomson came in too low . . . and a gust of wind forced his plane onto [the hangar's] canvas roof. His wheels sunk well into the roof,*

*but instead of somersaulting, he just bounced off and made a second
landing on the ground. Somehow it looked perfectly normal.*

With his new RFC squadron in France, between his assignment in
August of 1917 and the end of the year, he was promoted to captain and
made a flight commander in spite of his youth. He seems to have not
taken seriously either the war or his part in it, as he was called "cheerful"
Thomson. He flew Sopwith Pups to start, and then the deadly, dangerous
Camel, and in March of 1918 he ran up a total of fifteen victories—
including four in a single day—and won the Military Cross.

His time in combat included at least two encounters with the von
Richthofen Circus, led by the Red Baron in person. They were a difficult
christening for the brand-new pilot, for they were his first two engage-
ments, and he was lucky to escape with a bullet-graze on his head and
sundry holes in his airplane.

The pivotal year of 1917 saw the turning of the tide against Germany,
but victory for Britain and her allies would be dearly won. That year,
according to one estimate, the average life expectancy for British pilots
was about six weeks, as the RFC carried the fight into the sky above the
German line in its usual aggressive style, bucking not only Germany's
best pilots but often their superior aircraft, and always the prevailing west
wind, which made it difficult and sometimes impossible to fly a wounded
bird home to the safety of the British lines.

At length he was moved back to England as a trainer, to the outspoken satisfaction of his hometown neighbors, inspiring the *Helensburgh
and Gareloch Times* to trumpet proudly:

*A vast amount of satisfaction has arisen in the town, especially
amongst those who took a leading part in the welfare of the Helensburgh Swimming Club, that one of their number, now Captain
George Thomson, KOSB RAF has the proud distinction of wearing
the ribbon of the DSO, also the ribbon of the Military Cross. . . . As a
swimmer he was in the front rank of the many young men who were
members of the club.*

The paper went on to congratulate Thomson and wish him good luck, but that was not to be. For on the afternoon of May 23, he was flying his Camel from Norfolk to a field in the Midlands of England and made a routine landing at an RFC field called Port Meadow, near Oxford. All he wanted was a tank of gasoline, and he duly received his fill. An account of his arrival in the *Oxford Journal* reported his arrival and departure, adding this somewhat cryptic comment: "Before starting the machine was tested and found to be in order."

Whether this entry reflects no more than the routine walk-around good pilots often made during a break in a flight, or whether it indicated some unusual concern on Thomson's part, will always remain an open question. What is certain is that as his Camel climbed away from Port Meadow, it seemed to burst into flame at about six hundred feet, an accident later chalked up to a probable carburetor backfire. The Camel then dropped out of sight. As it did, Thomson seemed to be side-slipping the fighter, a measure that might have helped to keep the flames away from the cockpit.

As many other pilots did, Thomson himself had nightmares about dying in a "flamer," an aircraft on fire in the air, and at least once he had a nightmare about it so vivid and violent that it had taken three men to wake him up.

When his body was found, it was badly burned, but a doctor opined that he had been killed by the impact of the crash. You have to hope so.

CHAPTER SIXTEEN

One Tough Irishman

George McElroy (RFC)

THE IRISH, 'TIS SAID, ARE A FIGHTING RACE, AND THAT PUGNACIOUS character was never more evident than during the two world wars. In World War II many citizens of the Irish Republic crossed over Ireland's border into Ulster and joined the British army—one whole platoon crossed together, following its sergeant. And in World War I many Irishmen fought happily and well for the Crown, and not only in the traditionally Irish regiments, like the Dublin Fusiliers and the elite Irish Guards.

Such a man was George McElroy, who grew up in Dublin's Donnybrook County. When the war broke out in 1914, McElroy enlisted in the Royal Engineers, later moving to the Royal Irish Regiment after he was commissioned. Like so many other men of the PBI—the "Poor Bloody Infantry"—he got a heavy dose of German mustard gas and was sent home while he recuperated. That was April of 1916, the time of the Dublin riots and rebellion called the Easter Rising. Like many other Irishmen who fought for the Crown, he refused to take up arms against the rebels—he would not fire on other Irishmen—and was moved away from Dublin.

He was then sent as a cadet to the Royal Military Academy, from which he emerged as a second lieutenant of artillery, almost immediately becoming a pilot trainee in the RFC, and was sent to 40 Squadron in France, where he had the invaluable on-the-job tutoring of Mick Mannock. He flew an SE5 to his first victory late in the year, and then there was no stopping him.

He was an aggressive pilot who seemed to care little about the odds against him, much like Albert Ball, and by April 7 he had run his score to twenty-seven, a mixture of aircraft and balloons, but that day he caught a treetop during a landing. He survived, but required some mending time. He was at it again in June, during which he ran his score up to thirty, but that was only a prelude to a spectacular July, during which he had seventeen more kills and an emergency landing he survived with "scratches and bruises."

He was so bold in combat that even Mick Mannock warned him, taking him aside at a farewell lunch for mutual pal "Noisy Lewis": Don't follow a Hun down within easy range of ground fire, Mannock said. Good advice, that, but McElroy didn't heed it, nor, in the end, did Mannock. Before the month was out, Mannock went too low, and his brilliant career was ended by enemy fire from the ground.

By now holder of two Military Crosses, McElroy lasted less than a week longer than his friend Mannock, for he remained aggressive and careless of his own safety. Flying his second sortie of the day—he got his forty-seventh victory on the first run—he simply disappeared. Only later was it learned that he had been shot down and killed, like Mannock, by ground fire.

After his death he was awarded the Distinguished Flying Cross to go with his two awards of the Military Cross. His brief, meteoric career had been a fitting end for a man, an honorable warrior who once refused an order to fight.

WORLD WAR II

STILL ANOTHER WAR TO END ALL WARS

AFTER A CELEBRATED—AND BADLY BUNGLED—PEACE TREATY, AN exhausted world felt it could at last set its sights on the future, a future most people in the west assumed would be a world of perfect peace. There were lots of speeches about it, mostly by sincere, good-hearted people who did not, or did not want to, understand that evil still persisted in the world, just as it always had.

One solution offered for continuing international tranquility was the League of Nations, a high-sounding collection of politicians who talked a lot, but by and large believed in neither guns nor guts. It sat in Geneva—and the operative word is indeed "sat"—and spent its days damning—politely, of course—the various vicious aggressors pushing other people and nations around all across the globe, but carefully avoiding actually doing anything definite that might impede them.

The result, through the crystal-clear lens of hindsight, was almost inevitable: the rise of a German madman, a pompous Italian dictator, and a collection of Japanese devotees of *Bushido*, the way of the warrior. And when the aggressors of the world came to try their hand at pushing peaceful folk around, they found themselves at first opposed by clouds of hot air and very little else.

Aggression by aggression, getting bigger and bigger and worse and worse, the storm clouds began to form over east and west. Those who tried to keep the peace by talking sincerely with the aggressors were rewarded by smiles and perfidy. Although hopeful politicians assured the world that the millennium had come, in the end there would be no "peace for our time," in Neville Chamberlain's fatuous phrase spoken on his return from the Munich capitulation to Hitler in the autumn of 1938. He also used the phrase "peace with honour," an even less accurate, even more shameful mischaracterization of the Munich surrender.

What Chamberlain and Daladier of France achieved at Munich was to unwittingly open the path of Europe to bloody war; they left the Munich conference without a shred of their honor left.

When it finally broke, this second world war would prove to be even worse than the first one, not only in the efficacy of the weapons used, but in particular because of the accompanying mass murder by the Axis powers and their foul treatment of prisoners of war, especially in the Far East.

So the job had to be done all over again, in rivers of blood, with millions of shattered lives. And once more, America and Britain and their flying aces would take the lead down the very long, very tough road that led at last to peace once more. Now we have the United Nations, at times just as feckless as the League was, an empty suit, an entity, as the Indian chief said, "heap big smoke and no fire." We are told that at least today the people who genuinely want peace are more alert to international dangers and threats than they once were. We can only hope that is true, and that the free world's leaders will not only recognize a clear and present danger to our way of life, but have the courage to defend it. Look at what happened before.

CHAPTER SEVENTEEN

A Man of Dash and Gallantry

Robert Stanford Tuck (RAF)

As a youngster, Bob Tuck got started in life somewhat slowly. Born in the summer of 1916 in Catford, South London, he managed to get through school with a profoundly disappointing record until he left Catford's St. Dunstan's College in 1932. He went from the halls of academe to become a sixteen-year-old sea cadet, going to sea on the SS *Marconi*. That career path changed two years later, when he signed up with the RAF for a "short-service" commission as an acting pilot officer.

Tuck successfully completed his courses in the air and on the ground, and after a series of "acting" probationary appointments became Pilot Officer Tuck in 1936. The next year he was promoted to flying officer and, three years later, sent down to 92 Squadron, then based at Croydon. That was in May of 1940, a year in which England had need of every one of her sons. Germany was on the march, and the power of the *Luftwaffe* had already been demonstrated.

Tuck came to the war before the month of May was out, leading a patrol over Dunkirk and claiming three German fighters destroyed. The following day he added two bombers, and from then on his score grew rapidly. Bob Tuck had found his place in life, and was awarded the Distinguished Flying Cross on the 11th of June. The citation cited his "great dash and gallantry." He was now leading his squadron, thanks to casualties among his seniors in fighting against huge odds. The DFC citation recognized another patrol in which Tuck led the remaining eight

Spitfires of the squadron against a massive German formation of fifty aircraft, after fighting off a Luftwaffe formation of sixty the day before. The squadron claimed ten enemy shot down during these two fights, plus another twenty-four "possibles."

On and on the fight went, through the long summer of 1940, and Tuck's score continued to mount. On the 18th of August, however, after shooting down one Junkers Ju 88 and damaging another, he had to bail out after he was hit by a cannon round from yet another Ju 88 while making a head-on attack on the bomber. He was back in the air immediately, and only a week later he shot down a Dornier bomber some fifteen miles off the English coast. Hit during his attack, he lost his engine, and had to nurse his fighter back to a successful dead-stick landing in England.

In mid-September, with the Battle of Britain raging, he was promoted to flight lieutenant and acting squadron leader, and sent to command 257 Squadron, which flew Hawker Hurricanes. The Battle of Britain began to peter out in the latter days of September, and by the end of the next month, the German initiative was losing its steam, emerging as a clear British victory. It had been, as the Duke of Wellington said of Waterloo, "a close-run thing."

Tuck's score continued to mount: Ju 88s, a Messerschmitt Bf 109, and a Messerschmitt Bf 110. The 109 was probably the famous German ace Hans-Joachim Marseille. The German was hit in about that place at about that time, and bailed out of his fighter over Cap Gris Nez and was rescued by a Heinkel float plane.

The next month Tuck won the Distinguished Service Order, the citation crediting him with four enemy aircraft, and in a second award of the DSO in March, he was given credit for four more, running his total score to twenty-two. His career was somewhat further delayed in June when he was shot down over the Channel and fished out of the water by a Gravesend coal barge.

One more piece of bad luck awaited Tuck when he attacked a German bomber near Cardiff, Wales. The German dumped his bomb load in open country instead of on the city, a blessing for the city but not for an army training camp, which took one of the bombs. Only a single soldier was killed, but that soldier was Tuck's brother-in-law.

In July of 1941 Tuck was elevated to acting wing commander, flying fighter missions over northern France. With a brief break to visit America and plug Britain's war effort, he returned to Biggin Hill air station—now a wing leader—to lead so-called rhubarb missions over France. A rhubarb mission's whole point was simply to go across the Channel and shoot up anything German: trains, planes, fortifications, vehicles, bridges, and troops, but it had its accompanying hazards, for extremely low-level attacks attract angry anti-aircraft fire in large quantities.

So it was with Tuck: His Spitfire took a dose of flak that forced him to crash-land.

He was captured of course, but he was captured by some of the same troops he had just been shooting, which was not a good thing. Fortunately, their anger cooled at the discovery that one of Tuck's 20mm rounds had struck the barrel of a 20mm cannon on the German side and had ruptured its barrel like "peeling a banana," a fact the Germans found to be intensely amusing. Instead of more anger, it provoked comments like "Good shooting, Tommy!" and Tuck passed undamaged into captivity.

Over the next years he passed from camp to camp in Poland and Germany. He tried several times to escape, unsuccessfully, until on the 1st of February, 1945, he and a Polish pilot with an unpronounceable name successfully got away as their camp was being moved west ahead of the Russians. Since Tuck's nanny had been Russian, he retained some of the language, and he was able to communicate with the local people, even, one story says, fighting beside them. In time he found his way to the British embassy in Moscow and was on his way home.

In May of 1949 he retired from the RAF with the permanent rank of wing commander, taking with him one last decoration, the United States Distinguished Flying Cross. In the complex scoring system the RAF used, his final record was twenty-seven kills and two more shared with others; one and one probable unconfirmed destroyed; six probably damaged and another share. Somewhat later he was given credit for a full thirty kills.

In 1953 he and his wife moved with their two sons to a farm in Kent, where he happily and successfully raised mushrooms for more than twenty years. He was not eager for publicity, but did work as a technical advisor on the superb film *The Battle of Britain*. He became a close friend of another technical advisor on the same film, legendary German pilot Adolf Galland, a friendship strong enough that Tuck became godfather to Galland's son Andreas.

Robert Stanford Tuck passed away in 1987, at the age of seventy. A plaque to his memory in the Parish Church of St. Clement in Sandwich, Kent, says it all about his life:

> *A courageous officer who defended this nation in the*
> *skies above Kent during the Battle of Britain in 1940 . . .*

CHAPTER EIGHTEEN

The Man with the Tin Legs

Douglas Bader (RAF)

DOUGLAS BADER HAD BEEN A BRILLIANT PREWAR ACROBATIC PILOT, chosen to compete on the Royal Air Force team at the Henley meet, the Olympus of competitive flying. He was also a champion at rugby and cricket, a good-looking youngster who fluttered a lot of hearts among the ladies.

But then, on the 14th of December, 1931, flying across a runway right on the deck—in a right-angle bank with his wings at the vertical— he caught a wingtip, and his little Bristol Bulldog biplane clobbered in. Providentially, his harness kept him in the cockpit and the airplane did not burn, but when frantic ground personnel pulled him from what little was left of the airplane, he was nearly dead; the ambulance dashed to the hospital with an attendant holding Bader's femoral artery closed with his fingers. Among other things, both legs were so badly damaged that they required amputation.

That would have been the end of a flying career for the ordinary man, for although the RAF passed him as capable to fly, the best government bureaucracy would do was a ground job. For a man with Bader's temperament, that simply was not good enough. His courage and determination would not admit defeat in a profession so important in his life.

Happily married and playing professional-level golf in his spare time with his new artificial legs, he left the RAF for a while and worked for an oil company, but his heart remained, as Lord Tennyson put it, "in the central blue." And with the outbreak of war, Bader asked to return to active duty. This time, with every experienced pilot needed to turn back the German attacks on Britain, he was returned to flight status, and soon rose to command a squadron of fighters. Although his concentration was on teaching and leading his young pilots, and getting them home safely again, he still had twenty-two confirmed victories.

He rose to wing commander, leading three fighter squadrons in the fighter sweeps over the Continent that followed victory over the Luftwaffe in the 1940 battles above England. The sweeps were aggressive sorties, gaggles of fighters out looking for trouble, taking the war to the enemy's own ground, fighting anything that would fly and fight, strafing anything on the ground of military use.

But then in August 1941, Bader went down over Le Touquet. Bader said later he thought that another aircraft had rammed him; legendary German fighter ace Adolf Galland thought one of his men had brought Bader down. Later research concludes that Bader's fighter was most likely downed by "friendly fire" in the wild confusion of the dogfight. He parachuted to safety.

Bader passed into captivity, again legless, since his artificial limbs had been badly damaged during his parachute landing. The Luftwaffe was sympathetic and humane, as were most of the German fighting services—as distinguished from the thugs of the *Gestapo* and the SS. His captors wined him and dined him and patched up his damaged legs as best they could, but the repairs left something still to be desired.

And so Galland arranged for a drop of a set of replacement legs by the RAF, flying in to drop them at a particular spot under a safe-conduct pass. Bader told Galland just what should be passed on to his wife, precisely where his spare legs were parked in their home. Also on Bader's list was a decent uniform and a new pipe, replacing the one that had been broken in the crash and was now patched together with tape.

Galland and his pilots entertained Bader, "lavishly," as one account put it. He was even allowed to sit in the cockpit of Galland's own Messerschmitt Bf 109, and there was much conversation about the relative merits of the 109 and the Spitfire. During a conversation with Galland,

Bader had the temerity to ask whether he could take the aircraft up, for "just one circle over the airfield."

"I nearly weakened," wrote Galland later.

Air Marshal Sholto Douglas got a telephone call from Winston Churchill, saying somewhat grumpily that

I see from the newspapers you've been fraternizing with the enemy, dropping a leg to a captured pilot.

Douglas had his answer ready:

Well sir, you may call it fraternizing, But we managed to shoot down eleven of the enemy for the loss of six or seven of our own, so I hope you might feel it was worth it.

It was good enough for the prime minister and, given Churchill's own spit-in-your-eye propensity for derring-do, probably warmed his heart.

Again relatively mobile, and with the respect of both his fellow prisoners and his captors, Bader might have lived out the war in the comparative comfort and safety of a Luftwaffe prison camp. But that sort of thing was not in Bader's personality, as enterprising and aggressive as it always had been. He was his country's man first, last, and always, the epitome of Winston's Churchill's statement in his country's darkest hour, "never give in. Never give in. Never, never, never, never!"

At first the Germans insisted on depriving him of his legs, and even carrying him to the latrine. That indignity infuriated him, and may well account for his abiding loathing for his captors, a detestation that continued throughout captivity, lending weight to his statement that "I am not one of those who regard war as a game of cricket."

Bader's temper did not improve when he was first lodged in a civilian jail. He caused such a ruckus over that, that he was moved to a Luftwaffe transient jail. He continued to be a monumental pain, testifying for the defense at a court-martial of the staff at the hospital from which he had escaped. He also became part of an escape party driving a tunnel under the wire. Because he wasn't much use for digging, he played "stooge," the lookout for interfering guard personnel.

In the end he was transferred to Oflag VIB, a dismal camp near Luebeck, full of other officers half-starved on insufficient rations . . . those that the guards did not steal. It came as a great relief when the camp closed down and everybody was moved by cattle car to a new, large camp at Warburg. Along the way other enterprising prisoners cut a hole in the car's floor and one by one escaped through it while the train was moving . . . until one officer misjudged the drop and was killed by the car's wheels.

At Warburg, Bader's favorite occupation was "goon-baiting," the gentle art of irritating the more obnoxious guards just short of getting beaten or shot; Bader was a past-master at the game. He also joined in still another escape attempt.

Just outside the wire was a shed used for clothing-issue. Bader and three others managed to go together to the shed; then, while other prisoners created a diversion, they slipped into an unused room—one of them picked the lock to get there. After full dark and another diversion to lure away the spotlights, they left the shed and walked down a lighted path past some German huts to freedom. The camp escape committee had equipped them with *Reichsmarks*, forged passes, maps, a compass, and homemade rations.

Ultimately their plan was frustrated by something beyond anybody's power to plan for short of divine intervention, a guard's pesky bladder. When the goon emerged to fix his pressing problem, he almost walked into the four prisoners and yelled for help. Back to camp.

Next in Bader's odyssey was a move to Stalag Luft III, at Sagan, between Breslau and Berlin. The business of escape-planning never missed a beat, this time with the added complexity of yellow sand lying beneath the drab surface earth; the sand was immensely tough to hide as you excavated a tunnel toward freedom. Bader could not help with the digging, but he elevated goon-baiting to a fine art. Finally the Germans had enough and told him he was to be moved. Predictably, he refused; no fewer than fifty-seven guards, all fitted out with helmets, rifles, bayonets, and all, appeared to escort Bader from the compound.

Bader would not push it further; he did not seem to care a great deal about his own safety—he never had; but a confrontation might end in other prisoners being killed or injured. And so he went along peacefully, even strolling through the ranks of guards as if he were inspecting them, to the intense amusement of the other prisoners. And so an oversize platoon of armed men managed to move a single, unarmed officer with tin legs. And as a finale, when the German guard wheeled to escort Bader to transport, fifty-six of them turned one way and one the opposite direction, to roars of prisoner laughter. It had been quite a show.

Bader survived another year of confinement, probably his hardest. In this, the last year of the war, Red Cross parcels no long arrived, and emaciation had shrunk the stumps of Bader's legs so that walking was both chore and agony. At last came the glorious sound of friendly shells exploding on the castle, announcing the approach of the Americans.

Bader hitched a ride back west with an American pilot and was warmly welcomed by a set of American officers. Their commander called to him: "Come on, Doug. I've got your wife on the phone."

Douglas Bader was going home.

Bader never forgot about other people who had lost limbs, and spent much of his time helping them. A foundation in his name continued to help the limbless long after Bader was gone. And Britain never forgot Bader, the sort of hero so dear to the hearts of the British people. In the autumn of 1945, he flew a Spitfire in the Battle of Britain commemoration fly-past, and was knighted in 1976 for his service to the disabled. He died of a heart attack in the autumn of 1982. Active to the end, he was on his way home from giving a speech at a Guildhall dinner honoring Sir Arthur "Bomber" Harris. Bader was honored with a memorial service at beautiful little St. Clement Danes Church on the busy Strand in London.

Among the mourners was a friend of forty years . . . German ace Adolf Galland.

CHAPTER NINETEEN

An Enigma

Pappy Boyington (US)

THE MARINE FIGHTER PILOTS GREGORY "PAPPY" BOYINGTON LED INTO battle from September 1943 to January 3, 1944, widely praised him, but he was vilified by many of the men he served with some seventeen months earlier. One comrade in the Black Sheep Squadron called him the best commander of any Marine fighter squadron during the war. Yet one member of Gen. Claire Chennault's Flying Tigers said that he had a great deal of respect for most pilots in that fabled group, but not Boyington.

He ignored his children, had four troubled marriages, and often failed to pay his debts, but at the controls of a Corsair in fall 1944, he was so skilled that *Life* magazine proclaimed him "born to be a swashbuckler."

The family he joined on December 4, 1912, veered toward destruction almost from the beginning of his parents' marriage. His father, Charles Boyington, was a two-fisted drinking dentist in Coeur d'Alene, Idaho; Charles divorced Gregory's mother, Grace (Gregory) Boyington a scarce seventeen months later, claiming with some justification that Grace had been unfaithful. She married her paramour, Ellsworth Hallenbeck, who gave young Gregory his last name (without a formal adoption) and moved them all to St. Maries, a small lumber town about twenty miles away.

This was not a happy home, even at Christmas. Gregory mainly remembered Christmas as a time when his relatives spent the day drinking, brawling, and fighting. He discovered a fondness for heights early in life and often climbed to high places.

While on a school playground at age five, he saw his first airplane, a biplane flying lower and lower toward a nearby field. The pilot was pioneer aviator Clyde "Upside Down" Pangborn, who had spent World War I teaching Army Air Service cadets at Ellington Field in Houston. While his classmates went back to the schoolhouse, Gregory ran toward the plane. Pangborn's widowed mother by then lived in St. Maries, while he toured the country for the last couple of years as a partner in the Gates Flying Circus.

Either Boyington's stepfather or mother came up with the five-dollar fee, and the next morning little Gregory stood in the open cockpit throwing handbills as Pangborn flew over, fascinating the local folks. He vowed to become a Marine after the husband of his second-grade teacher paid a visit to her classroom in dress uniform, and his high school yearbook noted his letters in wrestling and membership in a leadership organization and summed him up simply: "he can't be beat."

That fall he enrolled and began studying architecture and engineering at the University of Washington, Spokane. During a Sunday drive into Seattle, he chanced upon the Boeing Aircraft Company factory and got a close look at an F-4B fighter being prepared for the Marine Corps. To him, it seemed like a living being that he and only he should take to the sky. After switching his major to aeronautical engineering, he graduated in 1934, and discovered during a brief stint at Boeing that a desk job, even in aviation, was not for him.

The next April, now married with a child due the next month, he signed up for a new program training Marine and Navy pilots on salary. There was a catch, of course: After training he would be obliged to serve three years at cadet's pay, but then would receive a commission and a $1,500 bonus, worth some $26,000 in 2016 dollars. And there was a further catch: The program was open only to single men. Since he had recently discovered that his real name was Boyington, not Hallenbeck, he enrolled as a single man named Boyington.

His first solo flight at Pensacola Naval Air Station was on July 3, 1935; while there he quarreled with Capt. Joseph Smoak, a universally disliked instructor he would see again in the Pacific three years later. But from the beginning Boyington was nearly always comfortable in the air. While learning how to execute steep dives, he even adapted an old wrestling technique for keeping his head clear by tightening his neck muscles.

But on the ground sloppy paperwork, drinking, and the news that back in Seattle his wife had found someone else began to plague him. Eventually, these problems affected his performance in the air, causing an instructor to describe him as slow to learn, but a hard worker.

A year of Marine officer's basic school at Philadelphia didn't help matters. He finished third from the bottom in a class of seventy-three, but was assigned to the 2nd Marine Aircraft Group at San Diego in January 1939. While there he honed his fighter skills, competing in exercises against several future Medal of Honor winners, and qualified for carrier duty aboard the *Yorktown*.

Boyington's drinking and problems at home persisted; he was only free in the air, or so it seemed, until a new opportunity presented itself in faraway Asia.

Former Army Air Corps captain Claire Chennault, then serving as a colonel in the Chinese Air Force and part of a delegation sent to Washington in 1940, had advocated US assistance for the Chinese fighting Japanese forces then occupying about one-third of China. Despite military opposition, President Roosevelt secretly sent one hundred fighters to China and signed an April 1941 executive order authorizing US airmen to resign and fly from Burma against the Japanese as part of an American Volunteer Group (AVG), in the pay of the Central Aircraft Manufacturing Corporation (CAMCO).

CAMCO offered large salaries and promised bonuses for every Japanese fighter brought down. CAMCO seemed custom made for Boyington, who needed more money, and was burdened by a bad marriage and longing for adventure.

Now stationed back at Pensacola Naval Air Station, Boyington was one of many who listened to a CAMCO pitch at the San Carlos Hotel on August 4, 1941, and signed up for one year, with a verbal Marine Corps assurance that he could return to service. He left in mid-September. All CAMCO recruits registered at the St Francis Hotel in San

Francisco before the sea voyage west, listing their occupations in the hotel register as "missionary."

Despite such precautions, the American Volunteer Group was an open secret. By the time Boyington arrived to join nineteen other pilots waiting for a Wednesday, September 24 voyage to Burma, *Time* magazine and even Japanese radio had reported on the AVG mission. The Japanese broadcast predicted they wouldn't arrive.

The thirty-five-day voyage aboard the Dutch ship SS *Boschfontein* as "missionaries" was uneventful, although nightly blackouts served as a grim reminder of patrolling Japanese submarines that could sink them at any minute.

Real missionaries on the voyage, not knowing any better, made small talk with AVG pilots about the evangelistic challenges that awaited them. Boyington was asked to preach the first Sunday service on September 28 but begged off.

They filled the six-day cruise to Hawaii with booze and deck tennis, compliments of CAMCO. A few hours at the sprawling Royal Hawaiian Hotel on Waikiki Beach steeled them for the long voyage to Java, in present-day Indonesia, an intermediate stop before Rangoon, Burma. Along the way, Boyington enjoyed challenging drinking mates to wrestling matches, when he wasn't insulting the missionaries. They arrived on the war front at Toungoo, Burma, fifty days after leaving San Francisco. They encountered squadrons of mosquitoes the first night.

They trained at a British airfield with the understanding that the Flying Tigers would move on to China. With one war on their hands, the Brits wanted to delay war with Japan as long as possible. While there, as a member of the 1st Squadron, Boyington developed a close relationship with Olga Greenlaw, wife of the AVG executive officer; she saw him as a man only happy in the air, working on goals larger than himself.

His first meeting with former stunt pilot Claire Chennault initially impressed Boyington, but he didn't appreciate a 5:30 a.m. wakeup to begin a crash physical training course to toughen them up after the luxury booze cruise to Rangoon. Chennault also provided captured translated Japanese flying manuals, intelligence reports, and advice on Japanese tactics based on Chennault's analysis. The AVG pilots learned that Japanese pilots generally followed flight plans but often didn't improvise to meet unanticipated challenges.

To Chennault the key to fighting the Japanese Zero was getting close enough to exploit the light armor that made the Zero more maneuverable than their own bulky P-40s. Many of the pilots, including Boyington, had trouble landing them. Boyington challenged some of Chennault's tactical doctrines almost from the day of his arrival—particularly flying the fighters in threes—but in time became a proponent of Chennault's tactics, despite their troubled personal relationship.

They became Flying Tigers when pilot Charlie Bond spotted an Australian fighter sporting a crude tiger shark drawn on its nose in a British magazine. Another AVG pilot wrote Walt Disney and arranged for a more sophisticated insignia based on the Australian idea. Meanwhile, Boyington entertained the others by pulling rickshaws, wrestling cows, and other stunts when they weren't in training. By late November at least two pilots had been killed in training accidents, but the rest of the squadron was ready to fight.

Boyington and the others learned about Pearl Harbor soon after the attack, but days passed without orders to attack the Japanese airfield just two hundred miles away.

Eleven days after the surprise Japanese attack, Boyington and the rest of the squadron bounced through buffeting winds on the 670-mile flight to Kunming, China. They were pleasantly surprised to discover that the airfield barracks had many modern conveniences, including hot showers.

Boyington and the 1st Squadron began flying routine patrols, but went into combat action on January 26 over Rangoon. They were severely outnumbered, flying two thousand feet below attacking Japanese, two of whom pounced on Boyington from behind, soon joined by a third and then more. Boyington escaped by diving low and highballing for Mingaladon, Burma, with a Japanese bullet in his arm.

Three days later he was in the air again, this time with nine other Tigers who took down sixteen of twenty opposing Japanese fighters. Boyington later claimed two of them, although no official record supports him. *Time* magazine and others proclaimed the Tigers "knights of the air" even as Boyington stewed over his personal anonymity.

His first two confirmed kills came on February 6, in a dogfight one Rangoon citizen-observer described as something akin to rowboats attacking the Spanish Armada. Despite this, Boyington was passed over for a command slot, even as his relationships with his peers and supervisors eroded. He was bored by routine patrols, paperwork, and the other routine stuff that went along with flying combat missions. Worse still, he got drunk during a personal visit by Chinese leader Chiang Kai-shek and embarrassed Chennault.

As the Japanese came nearer, Boyington and some other AVG pilots flew to Magwe, some two hundred miles north of Rangoon. By late February the entire 1st Squadron moved to Kunming, China. Early the next month Boyington was blamed, justifiably or not, for leading five planes so far off course that they ran out of fuel and crash-landed near the Indochina border. He returned and personally piloted all five planes back to Kunming at great personal danger but lost his job as vice squadron leader anyway.

Boyington broke into another pilot's liquor at Kunming on March 20, but was sober enough four days later to help attack Japanese planes on the ground at Chiang Mai, Thailand.

Boyington and nine others lifted off from a field at Namsang, Burma, before sunrise on March 24. Later he claimed to have taken out seven planes on the ground; Chennault later decided to credit all participants for the total number of planes destroyed. As a consequence, on payday Boyington was credited for 1.5 kills, but claimed to the day he died he should have been credited for at least 2.5 Japanese planes that day.

Chennault claimed that the Flying Tiger raid on Chiang Mai succeeded through teamwork and superb tactics while urging the US government to replace the long outmoded P-40s with more modern airplanes. *Time* later compared the Flying Tigers to Knute Rockne's Notre Dame football teams.

Despite such praise the Flying Tigers were less than enthusiastic when Chennault announced in early April that they soon would be escorting British bombers and supporting the Chinese infantry, rather than hunting Japanese fighters on commission.

In the meantime Boyington had received word that he was being inducted into the US Army Air Corps July 1 despite earlier verbal assurances from the Marine Corps that this would not happen. He claimed that in fact, before resigning he'd been assured that he could be reinstated if he tired of China. This all but ended his Flying Tigers career. Boyington fell down a hill while inebriated, was hospitalized for two weeks, then tried to fly a P-40 while under the influence and showed up for night watch toasted. He resigned from the AVG on April 21 and returned home, having fully expected that Chennault would throw him out anyway.

Few if any Flying Tiger pilots regretted his departure. And Chennault did nothing at all to help Boyington get back in the Marines. Instead, he encouraged the Army to draft Boyington into the Air Corps and advised the Marines to reject him.

At home he discovered that his children had been placed in his mother's care due to his wife's neglect. After working several months in the same parking garage where he paid part of his way through college, he learned on September 3, 1942, that despite Chennault's advice, the Marines were reinstating him.

After another sea voyage and several months shuffling Marine paperwork, he flew some defensive patrols over Guadalcanal, shuffled more paper until August 1943, and then got a new plane and the assignment he'd been looking for.

The F-4U Corsair had arrived in February 1943. Designed to outspeed the Japanese Zero, it also protected the pilot and fuel on board much better than the enemy plane. Boyington particularly admired the shallow angle of climb the Corsair offered. But when could he get back into action? Boyington's old friend, Brig. Gen. James "Nuts" Moore solved that problem after running out of other options. Adm. William Halsey, commander of the Pacific, needed air support for his offensive in the Solomons. Halsey's ideal solution was an aggressive fully trained Marine squadron commander with an impeccable record, but none were available.

Moore recommended that the VMF-214 Marine Fighter Squadron now on R&R in Australia following the combat death of its commander now be led by Boyington. Moore's boss, Maj. Gen. Ralph J. Mitchell, commander of the 1st Marine Aircraft Wing, was aware of Boyington's quirks but took a chance on him anyway.

The squadron was an eclectic group, but not the collection of misfits and criminals portrayed years later in the television series *Baa Baa Black Sheep*. Many had attended prestigious colleges including Princeton and Notre Dame. Others had extensive combat experience. The squadron did have its share of eccentrics: One, 1st Lt. Christopher L. Magee, flew into combat wearing a swimming suit, bowling shoes, and a bandana.

Boyington was not the oldest of the lot—that distinction belonged to thirty-four-year-old Frank Walton, the former Los Angeles police officer now in charge of squadron intelligence. And when Boyington arrived, Walton was assigned to keep him off of booze and out of trouble.

Soon after arriving in August, Boyington challenged the entire squadron except tall rangy Walton to wrestle him. When sober, Boyington pondered a serious problem. Eighteen of the twenty-four or so squadron pilots had no combat experience.

During their first meeting he compared the strengths and weaknesses of the Zero and the Corsair, emphasized the importance of staying with the squadron instead of pursuing Zeros lone-wolf style, and helped them visualize the tactics they would use in dogfights. He taught them how to confront and use fear, seek safety in numbers, and live to fight another day by resisting the often lethal temptation to do victory rolls over enemy lines. Whatever they had heard about his drunken rampages and misadventures, the young pilots around him at this first meeting showed Boyington nothing but respect. A leader, however flawed, was born that day.

Facing combat in the near future, the squadron had only a few weeks to prepare, unlike those in their wing who had trained as much as a year stateside. Boyington scavenged beat-up, worn-out Corsairs anywhere he could find them, and quickly put his men in the air on training missions, some of which ended with close calls. Robert McClurg made one landing with palm tree branches in his landing gear but became an ace with five confirmed kills.

The squadron was officially designated VMF-214 on September 7. That night or soon after, someone proposed they be called "Boyington's

Bastards" over drinks. A chairborne Marine publicity officer turned that one down but approved "Black Sheep" squadron. Marine combat correspondent Penn Johnson sketched out their insignia.

They landed at Henderson Field on Guadalcanal six days after being officially organized. Plane shortages meant that individual pilots took whatever Corsair was available for the daily mission. The first Black Sheep missions were escort duty protecting B-24 Liberators in an unchallenged airfield strike on Bougainville, followed by a photo reconnaissance mission plagued by Corsair oxygen, manifold, and brake problems. But the combat action some of the Black Sheep longed for would greet them soon enough, on their third mission.

The target was Ballale, a small island near Bougainville sheltering Japanese anti-aircraft guns. Some one hundred American planes left Henderson that Thursday afternoon, September 16, to take them out. Everyone on the flight knew that enemy fighters would do everything possible to bring as many of them down as possible.

"Tally ho!" someone yelled into the radio, just before some thirty Zeros filled the air space above the Ballale airfield, as the mostly combat-green Black Sheep pilots began the "spot, fire and evade" tactics that with some luck, might keep them alive. More than one of the newbies used the snap roll—a full-throttle dive technique Boyington had taught them—and survived to fight another day.

Boyington's first kill that day mistook him for a comrade, waggled his wings, then paid with his life. According to Boyington's action report, he scored his second victory at ten thousand feet. The Zero exploded about fifty feet away from his Corsair. Boyington climbed again, this time to eighteen thousand feet. While there he attacked a Zero that climbed, rolled on its back, and exploded. His fourth kill of the day was a trick shot; he'd been lured after one Zero, but turned and shot down the one that had been following him just the way Chennault taught him two years earlier.

He became an ace a few months later, while rescuing another American from two Zeros at about ten thousand feet, then landed at Munda, an American airbase on New Georgia Island in the Solomons, with only ten of the 237 gallons of fuel he started with.

Back at Banika where they started, he learned that all told the Black Sheep had eleven confirmed and nine probable air victories over Ballale, but Capt. Robert T. Ewing was never seen again. Daily but largely uneventful missions during the next eleven days ended on a return flight from a September 27 bomber escort mission to Kahili, near Buin on Bougainville. While returning, Boyington and six other Black Sheep pilots encountered fifty Japanese planes. He picked a Zero, went in for a confirmed kill, bagging one of four Black Sheep scores that day, but Lt. Walter Harris was lost.

And with that the small but formidable Marine public relations machine went to work, describing Boyington as "a man on his way to becoming a living legend." Soon a reporter arrived to feature Chicago-area Black Sheep, including bandana-wearing Lt. Christopher Magee, in a series of articles. He photographed several of them on September 29, the day they lost one of the best Black Sheep pilots, Lt. Robert Alexander, in a friendly fire incident near Munda. They had flown seventy-five missions in September, but more challenges were ahead.

Despite constant maintenance problems the Black Sheep and other Marine squadrons kept their Corsairs in the air throughout October, preparing the ground for large-scale attacks to come the next month.

"Major Boyington, what is your position, please?" someone asked in an accented voice over the radio on October 4, while Boyington and six other Corsair pilots were protecting dive-bombers attacking Kahili. He gave a fake position, then patrolled nearby in ambush with his squadron. Within sixty seconds Boyington scored three Zeros.

Boyington added one more to his score on October 15 in another attack on Kahili. He bagged a Zero trio in sixty seconds on October 17, when some forty Zeros rose from the airfield at Kahili the next day to attack several Corsairs the Black Sheep Squadron was using as bait. After that Boyington personally strafed the Kahili airfield, and then led the squadron back for another run in which he personally took out one of the eight Zeros destroyed.

The first six-week Black Sheep tour ended on October 19. By that time American flyers had significantly reduced the number of experienced Japanese fighter pilots still in the air.

Boyington's claimed six kills in Burma combined with fourteen confirmed kills in the South Pacific. Another Marine aviator, Joe Foss, also had twenty kills, which prompted the American press to promote a competition between Boyington and Foss to Boyington's regret.

The Marines published a January 1944 booklet highlighting sixty-four points for combat pilots taught by Boyington but compiled by the Black Sheep Squadron members, rather than Boyington himself. He compared air combat to boxing matches in which the fighters maneuver strictly by reflex. Black Sheep pilots memorized the purpose of every Corsair knob and control as well as the strengths and weaknesses of the Japanese Zero. Through example Boyington taught his pilots and hundreds of others that despite its supposed invincibility, the Zero could be destroyed. He was a natural-born teacher where killing was concerned. Lt. Harold E. Segal, a pilot from another squadron, later recalled how Boyington had saved his life by teaching Segal a specific maneuver during an evening bull session.

During a six-day R&R trip to Australia, he bumped into his old nemesis from Pensacola, Lt. Col. Joseph A. Smoak, who tried to have Boyington transferred out of his squadron. Instead, thanks to a Boyington admirer, Smoak was transferred to the same chairborne, nowhere assignment Smoak had planned for Boyington.

On November 27 the Black Sheep Squadron flew into Vella Lavella, an insect-plagued island a scarce seventy-five miles southeast of Kahili, the Japanese airfield they'd been attacking since September. The ultimate Solomon Islands target was Rabaul, some 225 miles farther.

Boyington and seven other Black Sheep led seventy-six other aircraft in a December 16 search-and-destroy sweep to Rabaul, an attack he and his boss, General Moore, had been arguing for since September. Although only eight Japanese aircraft were destroyed, four days later Boyington led forty-eight Corsairs back to Rabaul, trailing behind American bombers used as "bait" to bring up Japanese Zeros.

This time "Gramps," as some of his men now called him, dispatched one target from only fifty feet away, climbed to ten thousand feet for a second score on a Zero in mechanical difficulty, then dropped a third Zero circling the spot where the second dropped into the ocean.

His fourth kill of the day came minutes later as Boyington charged yet another formation patrolling at ten thousand feet, but was then chased into Vella Lavella by eight Zeros. The squadron began Christmas celebrations the next evening, complete with a whiskey-laced eggnog concoction.

As the daily fighter sweeps continued, Boyington downed his twenty-fifth claimed kill two days after Christmas. Newsmen now greeted him each time Boyington returned to Vella Lavella, waiting for word that he had set a new record. He hoped to get there by the time his second tour ended in early January, but was beginning to wonder whether that would happen, even though Boyington was flying two missions a day dead-tired, confiding in one letter that getting killed was the least of his worries.

He volunteered for a January 3, 1944, mission to Rabaul, and dived on a Zero from twenty-two thousand feet, to tie Rickenbacker's record. Boyington's wingman, George Ashmun, screamed, "Gramps, you got a flamer," just before Ashmun himself was surrounded and shot down by Zeros. A postwar report filed by Boyington and Black Sheep Squadron pilot Frank Walton stated that Boyington flamed two more Zeros trying to protect Ashmun, who crashed into the water near Rabaul and was never heard from again.

Boyington was now in trouble himself, sustaining shrapnel wounds even as his fuel tank exploded. Later he recalled parachuting out just before the crash as everyone else returned to base. Within hours the Black Sheep were in the air looking for him, from New Ireland to New Britain, to Bougainville, searching airfields, harbors, supply dumps, and anywhere else Boyington might be hiding. They flew their last mission as the Black Sheep Squadron on January 6.

Rumors in the days that followed placed Boyington among twenty aviators harbored by natives, on his way through Saipan to Japan, or, as his friend Frank Walton feared, executed by the Japanese. *Time* magazine reported him dead on February 21; the squadron was in effect disbanded on March 1 when the fifteen remaining Black Sheep were sent elsewhere.

Two weeks earlier on February 16, Boyington and five other prisoners were flown out of Rabaul on a Japanese bomber, only to be nearly killed during a massive American naval air attack on Truk, a base in the Caroline Islands. He'd been saved by Japanese navy interpreter Edward Honda, who had grown up in Hawaii.

The next stop was Ofuna, the notorious island prisoner of war camp near Yokohama described later by an American captive as "one big crime." Louis Zamperini, later made famous by the film *Unbroken*, was also a prisoner there at the time. During the five months Boyington was missing, the press continued to report on his possible whereabouts, including a May 1944 *Chicago Daily Tribune* article that compared him to French ace Georges Guynemer, who simply disappeared during a World War I mission. For the most part, the press and public assumed Boyington was dead; the president awarded him the Medal of Honor in March 1944.

But he was still alive. Despite intense interrogations, his living conditions improved markedly in September 1944 when he was assigned the best job in the camp, working in the kitchen, perhaps with Honda's help. Boyington was also sober for the first time in years, unable to indulge in the off-duty drinking he'd enjoyed while not flying combat missions.

February 1945 brought a full-scale air strike against the Yokosuka naval station some twelve miles from Ofuna. The prisoners watched the action with excitement and more than a little fear. Two months later he was transferred to an equally dismal island camp at Omori as a "special" prisoner. These captives, mostly pilots, received fewer rations and none of the "privileges" enjoyed by other inmates.

As American bombings increased, the Omori prisoners began excavating caves some six miles from the camp. An inadvertent stumble on the way back brought a beating, but Japanese civilians sometimes did what they could to help the Americans, sneaking them food or dropping cigarette butts to be easily found and picked up.

Boyington, pugnacious bulldog that he was, couldn't resist baiting the guards from time to time. He once hit one with a squash without suffering any reprisal. Some Japanese guards courageously cared for the Americans. One, known to history only as Kano, snuck several special prisoners to American doctors located elsewhere in the prison for medical treatment.

Boyington later described the ever-increasing bombing of nearby Yokohama as "music." Yet it was music that caused untold thousands of rats to swim from the mainland over to the prisoner island holding the Americans, as August 6, 1945, grew closer.

That day meant nothing in particular to the guards or prisoners at Omori, until word arrived that just after eight that morning the Americans had dropped an atomic bomb on Hiroshima, killing or mortally wounding between 90,000 and 160,000 Japanese. After a second atomic bomb was dropped on Nagasaki, many Omori prisoners concluded that they would be killed.

Boyington, now held prisoner for twenty months, was one of those who dreamed about surviving. And survive he did, liberated on August 29. Four days later Boyington and the other liberated Allied prisoners watched five hundred American bombers do a slow ceremonial fly-over commemorating the victory.

He arrived back in San Francisco September 12 and met his buddies at the St. Francis Hotel for a night of revelry marking his reunion with an old friend: booze. He briefly celebrated at the St. Francis and elsewhere in San Francisco before being swept away by well-wishers.

On October 4, 1945, in Washington, Boyington and Black Sheep Squadron intelligence officer Frank Walton filed a supplemental report, officially accepted by the Marine Corps but nevertheless controversial to this day. Walton confirmed that Boyington knocked down three Zeros on January 3, 1944, rather than the sole kill reported during the war. Those two extra kills weren't mentioned in the Medal of Honor citation President Truman conferred upon Boyington at the White House the next day, but Boyington's claims of twenty-eight kills were challenged for the rest of his life.

Boyington's persistent drinking problem prompted the Marine Corps to retire him August 1, 1947, although he was not yet thirty-five. He drifted from love affair to love affair and job to job; he worked in a brewery, officiated wrestling matches, and bickered with the family he deserted over money.

"Pappy" staggered through the next thirty years without accomplishing anything. The 1958 publication of his memoir, *Baa Baa Black Sheep*, put some money in the bank, but led to the greatest controversy of his life.

Josephine Moseman, his fourth wife, was nudging him toward Alcoholics Anonymous when the first episode of the fictional television series loosely based on his memoir was broadcast nationally on September 21, 1976. During a Black Sheep reunion in Hawaii later that year, Boyington did something usually unthinkable. He apologized to everyone present.

One squadron member said that the television series only got one thing right: They flew Corsairs. Frank Walton, who corroborated Boyington's twenty-seventh and twenty-eighth kills thirty-two years earlier, complained that the NBC series had twisted significant war-making accomplishments into an inept travesty.

None of this kept Boyington from touring the country selling copies of his memoir at air shows. Sometimes he teamed with Masajiro Kawato, a Japanese pilot who claimed to be the man who shot Boyington out of the air. Other Japanese pilots acknowledged Kawato was in the battle, but said Kawato was flying cover at a higher altitude than the pilots who engaged the Black Sheep. By 1980 the barrel-chested swashbuckling bulldog who had been Pappy Boyington, plagued by medical problems self-inflicted and otherwise, was a mere shell of himself.

Worse still, a spring 1981 article by Robert Sherrod in *Fortitudine*, a newsletter of the Marine Corps Historical Program, argued Boyington's claimed twenty-eight kills should be reduced to 25.5 based on a document Sherrod discovered at Maxwell Air Force Base. Boyington responded in a published letter to *Fortitudine*, acknowledging the discrepancy in AVG records but blamed it on Chennault.

Bruce Gamble's definitive 2000 Boyington biography remarked that in the days following his August 29, 1945, liberation from Omori, he never mentioned the two extra kills the day he was shot down, but claimed them thirty-seven days later in his "supplemental" report.

The Boyington controversy has continued into the twenty-first century. Was he the underachieving swaggering braggart that some Flying Tigers made him out to be, or the skilled squadron commander who, despite his drinking excesses and exaggerations, led the Black Sheep through eighty-four days of combat downing ninety-seven planes, sinking twenty-eight vessels, and producing eight air aces?

Truth be told, he was both.

CHAPTER TWENTY

All-American Boy

Joe Foss (US)

Joe Foss was a winner, but he had to work extra hard for everything he got. Whatever the task was, he did it enthusiastically, with a grin. From his birth in a stark South Dakota farmhouse in the spring of 1915, life required a lot of him, and he never failed. He lost his father to an accident when he was seventeen, and with his mother and brother pitched in to make their hardscrabble farm pay. But at least from the time he watched a Marine Corps aerobatic team perform, his eyes were on the sky.

His brother, Cliff, took over running the family farm to permit Joe to finish high school and graduate from the University of South Dakota. Joe worked at a service station and bussed tables to pay tuition, and still found time to excel in three sports and serve as an enlisted man in an Army National Guard artillery outfit. As if that were not enough, he was part of a student group that advocated—and got—the university to establish a Civil Aeronautics Administration flying course.

By the time he graduated, he had logged some hundred hours in the air. In 1940 Foss had both a college degree and a pilot's license, and so he hitchhiked to Minneapolis to join the Marine Corps reserve, his path to the Naval Aviation Program. But after graduation the corps had decided that at the venerable age of twenty-six years he was "too old" to serve as a fighter-pilot, and assigned him to a photo reconnaissance unit. He was not pleased.

So, being Joe Foss, he bugged his superiors until he got his transfer to fighters. As a comparatively old fossil, he became executive officer of squadron VMF-121, and in October of 1942 VMF-121 embarked on an escort carrier and were catapulted off on a 350-mile flight to an obscure island in a Pacific chain few Americans had ever heard of. The island chain was called the Solomons. The island was Guadalcanal.

VMF-121 joined what was already known as the "Cactus Air Force," and they settled in, as far as any human being could, at what was called Henderson Field, named for Marine major Loften Henderson, killed at the Battle of Midway. Construction had been started by the Japanese, but was finished by Seabees and Marines. The rough strip was in a constant state of turmoil, what with Japanese aircraft overhead and regular shelling by the Japanese navy's big guns.

Joe Foss was right in his element. He was an aggressive pilot, given to closing to as short a range as possible, and his marksmanship was legendary. He brought down a Japanese Zero fighter on his first mission, but his Grumman Wildcat took its share of pounding and at least once required him to ditch at sea. Foss had the responsibility of leading his own flight of eight Wildcats, divided into two sections christened the "Farm Boys" and the "City Slickers."

Forced to take some leave time in Australia because of malaria, he was back on the job in early January of 1943. In about three months of combat, his little Circus made seventy-two kills; no doubt there were more than that, crippled Japanese aircraft that disappeared in the brutal jungle or the surrounding waters trying to reach their bases at Rabaul and elsewhere far to the north. Of the seventy-two confirmed Japanese aircraft, twenty-six were Foss's.

He returned to the United States in March, was lionized by the press, and received the Congressional Medal of Honor from the president. The ceremony was held at the White House, and Foss ended up on the cover of *Life*, which covered the ceremony. The story goes that the modest Foss was not comfortable as the center of all this fuss, and he was probably no more at ease on the victory bond tour that followed, but his score of enemy planes had equaled that of Eddie Rickenbacker, the American

"Ace of Aces" in World War I. But he had become a national hero; and orders, then as now, were orders, so on the tour he went.

By the following February he was back in action, leading a squadron of deadly gull-winged Corsair fighters. But this time there were many fewer chances for action; he had no chance to increase his victory score. It was not long before he was back in the United States, down again with malaria.

By August 1945 Foss was released from active duty and opened a business in Sioux Falls, specializing in flight instruction and charter flights. The operation grew to some thirty-five aircraft. In the next year he became a lieutenant colonel in the Air National Guard of South Dakota, commanding a fighter squadron, but during the Korean War he was recalled to federal active duty to become director of operations and training for Central Air Defense Command, in the course of which duty he rose to the rank of brigadier general.

He then served two terms as a Republican state representative—not surprisingly doing much of his campaigning from an airplane cockpit. And then, in 1955, he became South Dakota's youngest governor. He lost two elections after that and left politics to become the first commissioner of the brand-new American Football League. The league thrived under his leadership, and he stayed in the saddle until just before the merger of the AFL and NFL, a union that led to a superpower league and the now-classic Super Bowl.

Foss wasn't through. For three years he was the voice of ABC's popular *American Sportsman,* and served six years as director of public affairs for KLM Royal Dutch Airlines. Starting in 1988, Foss served two terms as president of the National Rifle Association, regularly speaking out in defense of the Constitution's Second Amendment, as he would do for years.

Charity played a large part in Joe Foss's life. Among his interests were the National Society of Crippled Children and Adults, Easter Seals, and the Campus Crusade for Christ. He and his wife founded the Joe Foss Institute, which sponsors youth education programs and scholarships. One source states that the institute, as of 2014, had assisted over a million kids.

There is almost no end to the list of Foss's activities—but they have one thing in common: All were aimed at helping other people and supporting the United States, the nation he loved so much and fought so hard to protect. He passed away on New Year's Day in 2003 of a stroke suffered some three months before. His funeral was attended by Vice President Cheney and NBC News anchor Tom Brokaw, among many others. A brief eulogy came from old friend Charlton Heston.

Brokaw captured the essence of Joe Foss in his 1988 book, *The Greatest Generation*:

> *He had a hero's swagger but a winning smile. Joe Foss was larger than life, and his heroics in the skies over the Pacific were just the beginning of a journey that would take him to places far from that farm with no electricity and not much hope north of Sioux Falls.*

Pretty fair epitaph.

CHAPTER TWENTY-ONE

Untiring Patience and Energy

Johnnie Johnson (RAF)

JOHNNIE JOHNSON WAS A LEICESTERSHIRE MAN, A UNIVERSITY-educated engineer, but from his boyhood he had looked more to the sky. He came of sturdy stock. His father was a police inspector who once went into a meeting of the British Union of Fascists who had overstayed their permitted meeting time. These brawling hoodlums were fond of violence, but Inspector Johnson broke up their meeting and threw them out . . . alone.

Johnson was a "principled" youngster—his brother's words—who loved sports and shooting, but also in his salad days expressed a passion for fast cars and what he called "pacey women." (I don't know what that means either, but I can guess.) In 1938 he broke a collarbone playing rugby and the setting of the bone was botched; it would plague him for years.

His ambition was to become an RAF pilot, but his path was not easy. He took flying lessons on his own, but he was initially rejected for pilot training. He was again turned down for a berth as a sergeant-pilot in the reserve; the Auxiliary Air Force was up to strength he was told, but there were openings in the balloon squadrons . . . but that was not Johnson's cup of tea. He wanted to serve his nation, and to him that meant a real military unit. He did not intend, he said, to spend the war "building air raid shelters or supervising decontamination squads."

And so he spent some time in a Territorial mounted unit, the Leicestershire Yeomanry. That was good, he thought, but he expressed his deepest desire one day on seeing some Hurricane fighters. "If I've got to fight Hitler," he said, "I'd sooner fight him in one of those than on a bloody great horse."

Finally accepted by the RAF in the summer of 1939, he successfully finished the flying instruction course, which earned him a commission and his pilot's wings on the same day. But the old collarbone injury and its bungled surgery returned to plague him again and again, so that he missed the airfighting from May to October of his country's heroic "backs to the wall" year of 1940.

Surgery at last fixed the collarbone problem. He returned to full duty in the first days of 1941, flying Spitfires, and began an almost incessant series of combat missions, some seven hundred of them stretching over the years 1941 to 1944. At first he flew as a night-fighter, but then joined the wing at RAF Tangmere, which was going flat-out on what Fighter Command boss Sholto Douglas called "Sector Offensive Sweeps," commonly known as "Circus operations." These were three-squadron affairs of several different types, low-level attacks, cover for bombers, and so on, but all of them shared one basic, highly pugnacious aim: fly into the heart of *Luftwaffe* airspace, then shoot people and break things.

On June 26 Johnson got his first kill, a Messerschmitt Bf 109. He had more victories in the nonstop fighting that went on all that summer and into the autumn. In the first week of September, Johnson was promoted to flight lieutenant and awarded the Distinguished Flying Cross.

That was a tough early summer for the RAF. The German Focke-Wulf Fw190, as Johnson put it,

was causing us real problems. . . . We could out-turn it, but you couldn't turn all day. As the number of 190s increased, so the depth of our penetrations decreased. They drove us back to the coast really.

But help arrived in midsummer in the form of the new Spitfire Mark IX, about the time Johnson got his second DFC and a promotion to squadron leader. He took command of 610 Squadron.

Early in 1943 Johnson took command of No. 144 Wing, mostly Canadian pilots, and his call sign, "Greycap," was a familiar sound in the air day after day. He scrapped the old "line-ahead" for the "finger-four" formation, a quantum jump in tactical flexibility and better protection against being jumped unaware by German fighters. And whenever he could, he ducked ground attack missions for his men, attacks which he believed wasted skilled, experienced pilots on targets of little value for little gain.

In July the USAAF began "Blitz Week," a concentrated dose of heavy daylight attacks. The Luftwaffe was up in force to defend, and the fighting was fierce. Johnson's pilots escorted the Flying Fortresses and Liberators, and Johnson knocked down three more Fw190s.

Johnson and his wing stayed on the offensive all through the summer of 1944, and in late August, climbing to recover altitude lost while shooting down two Fw190s, he decided to join a flight of six Spitfires. It was a prudent decision since he was flying alone, except that the six Spitfires turned out to be six 109s. Johnson made that almost-fatal discovery just in time to escape by some wild aerobatics, taking German cannon-fire as he twisted and turned.

His fighter was part of the heavy fighting over the failed raid at Dieppe, the Battle of the Bulge, and the invasions of Normandy and Germany. He flew in support of Market Garden, the historic multinational airborne strike that came so close to putting the Allies across the Rhine. His Canadians were a deadly, highly professional set of pilots, with a discipline and unity due, in large part, to what one of Johnson's medal citations aptly termed his "untiring patience and energy."

The last days of the war saw little action, for the battered Luftwaffe seldom came out to fight. As Johnson and his men went in to bounce a flight of four Fw190s, the German pilots' reaction was to waggle their wings, the airborne equivalent of surrender, and so Johnson's men simply escorted the four Germans to an RAF airstrip.

Johnson remained in the RAF after peace temporarily returned, and ultimately rose to air vice marshal. Along the way he served a tour in the United States and flew the Lockheed F-80 Shooting Star in action in Korea, winning a DSC, an Air Medal, and the Legion of Merit from America. His British decorations included three DSOs and two DFCs.

Besides these decorations and being anointed as a Companion of the Order of the Bath and a Commander of the Order of the British Empire, he finished his active service and worked as a fundraiser and speaker; after his retirement in 1966, he set up the four-thousand-property Johnnie Johnson Housing Trust. Otherwise, his chief passions were fishing, shooting, travel, and always . . . dogs.

After the 1982 death of his old boss and friend Douglas Bader, Johnson collaborated with two other Bader friends to continue helping Bader's passion, charities for disabled people.

Johnson died in 2001, aged a mellow eighty-five. He has a modest memorial on the grounds of the Chatsworth Estate, on which his ashes are scattered. It is a simple bench and the inscription on it is simpler still: "In Memory of a Fisherman."

Cold statistics can never tell the whole story of any man's achievements in combat, but Johnson's tally gives a pretty fair idea. He finished the war with a record of thirty-four individual victories, all fighters, plus seven more shared and three shared probables, plus more German aircraft damaged and another destroyed on the ground. More significant was the caliber of his opposition: His victories included fourteen Messerschmitt Bf 109s and 20 Focke-Wulf Fw190s, the best German fighter of the war.

Quite a record.

Quite a fighting man.

CHAPTER TWENTY-TWO

One-Armed Mac

James MacLachlan (RAF)

Squadron Leader James MacLachlan was a Cheshire man who signed on with the RAF at the minimum age of seventeen. By early 1939 he was a pilot officer, and when the German panzer spearheads smashed into France in May of 1939, he was a member of RAF Squadron 88, flying the Fairey Battle, theoretically a light bomber.

One veteran pilot is quoted as saying "only brave men fly Battles," a straightforward comment on an airplane that was a lethal failure. Though powered by the same tough Rolls-Royce Merlin engine that drove the Spitfire and the Mustang to greatness, with the weight of its crew and three-quarters of a ton of bombs, the best speed the Battle could crank out was still some one hundred miles per hour slower than that of the Messerschmitt Bf 109. On top of that, the Battle was pitifully underarmed, with only a single wing-mounted, forward-firing machine gun and another flexible .303 Vickers for the rear gunner.

The Battle squadrons regularly suffered hideous casualties. In one sortie twenty-four of them went out, and only fourteen returned. Another mission cost the RAF seven out of eight Battles; still another attack by five Battles ended with four of the light bombers destroyed and the fifth crash-landed on its home strip. And to cap it all, an RAF maximum-effort attack against the German Meuse River bridgeheads around Sedan—sixty-three Battles and eight Bristol Blenheims—ended with forty of the RAF attackers shot down . . . including thirty-five Battles. In just six weeks almost two hundred Battles were lost.

On June 15 the RAF pulled its last aircraft back to England. Thereafter the Battle was used against the shipping forming in the Channel harbors for Germany's Operation Sea Lion, sparingly against the Italians in east Africa, and lastly in Greece in the spring of 1941. The Fairey Battle had been a colossal failure . . . but worse still were the trained crew losses. You can always build more airplanes, but there are never enough able, dedicated, daring men to fly them.

James Archibald Finlay MacLachlan was a religious child, but he had his mischievous side, as one account of his days at school put it, by "forming libelous rhymes about his contemporaries and members of staff." He was deeply interested in wild animals and biology generally, but from the time he stepped into his first airplane—a short ride at a sort of open house held by the RAF at Leuchars—he decided he would be a Royal Air Force pilot.

He flew the omnipresent Tiger Moth early in March of 1937, then graduated to the Hawker Hart and Hawker Audax, both handsome but obsolescent biplane fighters, the Audax a variation of the Hart. Both were fast for their time and type, and good training for the Advanced Flying Training School, where MacLachlan learned close-support aviation, including dive-bombing.

His first operational steeds were the deathtrap Fairey Battles, the too-slow, under-armed poor excuse that got so many good crew members killed, and MacLachlan volunteered for Fighter Command, was selected, flew briefly on operations over Scotland, and was then assigned to Malta. And over that tiny, vital island in January 1941, he was in action, first against the Italians and then both them and the Luftwaffe. Flying a Hurricane, he became an ace the same month.

The RAF logged many hundreds of hours in the desperate, finally successful effort to keep the tough little island alive, taking on not only dozens of air raids on the island itself, but also heavy attacks on the supply convoys that were the lifeblood of the island's people and garrison.

The defenders knocked down German bombers and Italian fighters in large numbers, but the arrival of Messerschmitt Bf 109s was a blow to morale; the German fighter's performance was far superior to that of the aging Hurricane; "they left us standing," said MacLachlan.

And MacLachlan, in the thick of the fighting as usual, took a volley of German cannon-fire in his engine and cockpit. His left arm would not work, and he had to struggle to shed his helmet and radio gear, but he finally managed to get out of the doomed airplane. He almost gave up, he said later, until he thought of his mother reading the standard "regret to advise" telegram announcing his death.

He landed in a civilian garden.

I hurriedly tried to think up some famous last words to give my public, but I never had a chance to utter them. . . . I was surrounded by a crowd of shouting, gesticulating Maltese. . . . I had to give up the dying idea to concentrate . . . on kicking every Maltese who came within range.

That was the spirit of the man, and the story goes that MacLachlan's nurses and fellow-pilots were making bets that he would return to action within two weeks. They were right, in spite of having his left arm amputated below the elbow.

Back in England he was certified to fly—shades of Douglas Bader—and Queen Mary's Hospital carefully studied the layout of a Hurricane's controls and fitted him with a special prosthesis, a custom-built arm and hand that included four spring-loaded fingers giving him access to four specific controls. He flew as often as he could, and sported a special badge painted on the fuselage of his fighter: a human arm and hand giving the V-for-victory sign . . . with a large hole through the arm.

First flying night missions across the Channel, he and his mates strafed railroad stock and river transport, and targeted German aircraft bombing Britain; on the night of May 4–5, he trailed two Junkers Ju 88 bombers returning from a raid over England and shot both down over France. He and others flew many more night intruder missions, giving the German raider crews no place of safety. As usual, he made light of it:

The average intruder pilot is not the cat-eyed, carrot-eating killer that the press sometimes makes him out to be. . . . Most of us . . . are too fond of our mornings in bed.

Nevertheless, he and another pilot were idolized by the *Daily Express*—somewhat melodramatically—as "The Killers Who Stalk By Night," and he was assigned as an instructor, including an extended trip to the United States, teaching USAAF pilots in flight school from one side of America to the other, and enjoying American hospitality and celebrity status in Hollywood.

He was back in England in April 1943, and that same month brought him the bitter news that his brother Gordon had been shot down and killed over France while escorting B-24 bombers. MacLachlan agitated for a return to combat, and finally got it. Fighter Command boss Trafford Leigh-Mallory approved his return to what were called "Ranger" operations over France, a challenge for which he prepared with many hours of tree-top flight around England, his theory being that the deep penetration called for by Ranger operations was best done, as the RAF put it, at "naught feet."

His experiment was extended to Europe, and one memorable flight was made with RAF lieutenant Geoffrey Page, who had been shot down during the Battle of Britain and badly burned. Page wanted a German for each "of the 15 operations he had endured since 1940." Page, obviously a kindred spirit of MacLachlan, said of the mission, "fine bloody pair we are, going off . . . with only one good hand between us!"

One was good enough. Flying American P-51 Mustangs, on a single sortie they destroyed a flight of four Focke-Wulf trainers; for dessert that day they shot down two Ju 88 bombers. Luck like that, however, was not destined to last. Flying another two-fighter, zero-altitude run over France in July 1943, Page saw MacLachlan hit by ground fire, saw him pull up his Mustang, apparently looking for a place to bail out. Instead, he then tried to put the fighter down in a small field. He managed to hit his target, but skidded on into an orchard, which ripped off the aircraft's wings.

Page orbited the area looking for signs of life, but was disappointed, for MacLachlan was gone. There had been no call on the radio; there was no movement around the Mustang; but still Page contemplated landing and trying to pick MacLachlan up. Finally, he had to conclude that there wasn't enough space to put his airplane down and then take off again. He gave it up and returned to England.

MacLachlan was finished in any case, although he lasted thirteen days before dying of his wounds, which included a fractured skull. The Luftwaffe gave him a funeral, the ceremonies conducted by a German priest. French civilians heaped flowers on the grave, along with a sign that said, "He died that France might live." The Germans got rid of the sign immediately, but no doubt the sentiment lingered on. Both courage and gratitude are hard to kill.

MacLachlan finished his short career with three awards of the Distinguished Flying Cross and a DSO. Officially, he had credit for sixteen enemy aircraft shot down, one shared kill, and three damaged. His total was almost surely higher, but most important, then and afterward, was the example he set.

CHAPTER TWENTY-THREE

The Finest Natural Pilot I Ever Met

Richard Bong (US)

So said the flight instructor, captain, and future US senator and presidential candidate Barry Goldwater, who taught gunnery to young Richard Ira Bong and was quoting a journeyman fighter pilot's judgment of his prize pupil at Luke Field, Arizona. The judgment of the fighter pilot and Captain Goldwater would prove to be exact, for Bong would finish World War II as America's top fighter pilot, quite literally its ace of aces.

Dick Bong was the son of a farm couple who lived near the village of Poplar, Wisconsin. The size of Poplar can be measured by the size of its high school, which could only manage three grades. To finish up, he made a round-trip of more than forty miles to the comparative metropolis of Superior, which could manage four grades. From there he attended Wisconsin State Teachers' College. There he entered a government-sponsored aviation program and got his license in small planes.

The next step was to join the Army Air Corps' Aviation Cadet program, which sent him on in succession to Taft, California, and Phoenix, Arizona's Luke Field—perhaps prophetically. He was such a talented pilot that he was kept at Luke for three months as an instructor. By this time the United States had been in World War II for half a year and everything was in short supply, including fighter pilots and aircraft, so Bong was sent on to Hamilton Air Force Base across the bay from San

Francisco, where he trained on the brand-new twin-engine, twin tail-boom P-38.

Now young pilots tend to be bold and brash, eager to learn and excel, but also they tend, at least in western air forces, to be so full of beans that they are a pain in the kinonymous even to patient instructors. Bong was one of several youngsters who did things that tended to irritate both their superiors and the public generally. Bong's sins included flying loops around a span of the Golden Gate Bridge, the great engineering work across the narrows leading into San Francisco Bay, and flying low down San Francisco's Market Street, waving to the girls.

But what tore it with Maj. Gen. George C. Kenney, the commander of Fourth Air Force, was a complaint from a lady in Oakland—across the bay east of San Francisco—that one Monday Bong had buzzed her house and blown all her clean washing off the line onto the ground. What followed is related in several ways in several places, but the import of all the versions is precisely the same.

"Bong," said the general, "get over there and see this woman, and if she has any laundry to do, *you* will do it, and don't drop any or *you* can do it again. And hang around while the laundry dries and mow her lawn or something." And the general added this final adjuration: "I want this woman to think we are good for something besides annoying people. Now get out of here before I change my mind. That's all!"

Now anybody who's worn the uniform knows that when generals talk that way, it's good to be someplace else, or to be immediately on your way there, and to make yourself both meek and scarce thereafter. So Bong did, but what he could not know at the time was that General Kenney had marked him as the sort of officer that would fly and fight well, and when Kenney took command of Fifth Air Force out in Brisbane, Australia, Bong was one of fifty fighter pilots selected to go along.

He was attached temporarily to a squadron other than his own, for the unit to which he was first assigned was still flying the old Curtiss P-40. He was destined for the P-38 Lightning, then the class of Fighter Command. Bong's fellow pilots liked him, in spite of his antics above San Francisco, or maybe in part because of them. After all, they were kindred spirits. Besides, Bong was good company, quiet, even introverted, and he knew what was expected of a pilot in combat.

For two days after Christmas, he and his adopted squadron scrambled to meet a large force of Japanese Zero and Oscar-fighters and Val dive-bombers. The Vals descended on Buna, a New Guinea town newly taken by the Americans, and twelve American P-38s met them, led by Bong's trainer and friend, Capt. Tom Lynch.

Bong got two kills, a Zero and a Val, at one point in the dogfight pulling out of a dive, in his words, "two inches above the shortest tree in Buna," chased by no fewer than three Japanese fighters. The Val was a flamer, and Bong was on his way to aviation immortality.

Bong and his squadron mates met the Oscars of the Japanese Army and nailed six of them, Bong shooting one down after what was described as a "five-minute duel," an eternity during a dogfight. After a hurried refueling they were up again to meet another sixteen enemy fighters over Lae, and Bong shot another Oscar out of the sky. On the 8th of January, flying as escort to American B-17s and B-24s, Bong put in a frontal attack to help an American trying to hold off an aggressive Japanese Oscar. The Oscar exploded and dropped some eighteen thousand feet into the sea. That one must have been especially rewarding, for it was Bong's fifth victory, enough for ace status and, probably better still, a trip to Australia for R&R.

In what would be known to history as the Battle of the Bismark Sea, a large Japanese fleet approaching Lae, New Guinea, tangled with some three hundred bombers of both the American and Australian air forces. The fighting lasted parts of three days, and when it was over, the Japanese had lost nearly sixty aircraft, eight warships, and fourteen merchantmen. During the fighting Bong got one more kill.

The fighting continued on March 11, when the Japanese bombed the airstrip from which Bong's squadron was operating. Bong got off the ground just ahead of a stick of bombs, to find himself in a cloud of Zeros escorting the bombers. He sent two down on fire and another one smoking, but intelligently broke off his offensive when six more came at him. He returned to the airstrip on one engine. Before March was out, he had nine victories and brand-new first lieutenant's silver bars.

Bong was much given to head-on attacks, "close enough," as he put it, "to put the gun muzzles in the Jap's cockpit." At least sixteen of his wins came head-on, but he was also a thoughtful warrior, willing to break off a fight when things were not going well. And he had his own reasonable rules for the combat pilot, which he wrote down in a letter home, when one of his younger brothers was about to join the Army Air Force. They are well worth repeating here.

He must not get contemptuous of any airplane, no matter how easy it may be to fly. Don't just get in and fly it, but know what makes it tick . . . if he forgets, why, any airplane in the world can kill him if he isn't its complete master.

On the 12th of June, Bong got an Oscar, although the fighting cost him a badly shot-up P-38. And then, later in the summer, Bong had a field day, a quadruple kill of two Oscars and two Tonys (a nickname for the Kawasaki Ki-61). Four more of the enemy fell to Lt. Jim Watkins, who rejoiced in the nickname of "Duckbutt," and another pilot got two more of the Japanese, in spite of colliding with one of his victims.

Bong cut his performance a little fine in late August when he coaxed his shot-up P-38 back to a crash-landing; the airplane was a write-off, but Bong survived without injury. At this point General Kenney may have thought it was time to get his top ace out of the action for a little while. He sent Bong to the United States, where he had a chance to see his family and hometown friends.

Maybe even more important, he also met Marjorie Vattendahl, reigning homecoming queen at Wisconsin State Teachers' College. Bong became king of homecoming, and he and Marge discovered each other. It was apparently a real case of love at first sight, and once Bong returned to the South Pacific, he lost no time in christening his brand-new P-38J. The fighter became *Marge* and a portrait of the lady—maybe it was a photo—graced the P-38's shiny aluminum skin.

Bong flew when time and tactical reason allowed, for he was now on a very independent status as General Kenney's chief of replacement fighter aircraft. The kills of Japanese aircraft continued, and on March 5

Bong scored victory number twenty. On that very day, however, he lost a good friend with whom he frequently flew on his "roving commission" patrols. During a strafing mission, attacking Japanese barges and fishing luggers in Aitape Harbor, Bong saw his friend's P-38 hit by ground fire, and began to plead with his friend on the radio to jump, but had to watch helplessly as his friend's aircraft blew up at less than two hundred feet just as his friend struggled out of the cockpit.

Bong continued to fly his aggressive missions, and passed the all-time record of kills established by Eddie Rickenbacker in World War I. Rickenbacker sent his congratulations, and graciously added his hope that Bong would "double or triple this number." That would have to wait, for General Kenney, hearing that Bong was still flying extra long, hazardous missions, forbade him flying on missions except to see how his students were faring—he was now an instructor in "advanced gunnery"—and even then was not supposed to shoot unless shot at.

But the ultimate accolade was the Congressional Medal of Honor, which Bong received at the hands of General MacArthur. Bong continued to fly his aggressive missions, and General Kenney had enough. Dick Bong was going home, like it or not, as America's top ace, with a final score of forty kills, seven probables, and eleven damaged. He got a hero's welcome, and on February 10, 1945, he married his Marge before twelve hundred guests.

After the honeymoon Bong reported to his new assignment, Wright-Patterson Air Force Base in Ohio, to test-fly the new Lockheed P-80 jet fighter. After a little experience with the new airplane, he took it up for his eleventh flight, and something went very wrong. People near the runway saw puffs of black smoke from the plane's tailpipe as Bong reached three or four hundred feet; then the P-80 nosed down and went nose-first into the earth.

Witnesses saw the canopy fly off as the aircraft faltered, and Bong's body was found on the runway a short distance from the tarmac, with his deployed parachute wrapped around him. He had forgotten to activate the "takeoff and land" switch on his electric fuel pump before taking off, and his engine had quit during takeoff. At that low altitude no curative action was possible in the few seconds before the jet crashed.

Bong died loaded with his country's decorations for valor. Besides the ultimate award, the Congressional Medal of Honor, he held the Distinguished Service Cross, two Silver Stars, and seven awards of the Distinguished Flying Cross. In the Richard I. Bong Memorial Center in Superior, Wisconsin, however, is the memorial Bong would probably have liked best. It is a restored P-38, the airplane Bong flew to glory.

On its side is his favorite picture: his wife Marge.

CHAPTER TWENTY-FOUR

The Greatest Flying Ace

Pat Pattle (RAF)

BORN IN SOUTH AFRICA THE YEAR WORLD WAR I BEGAN, PAT PATTLE followed in the footsteps of his father, a sergeant-major, who enlisted at the age of fifteen and fought in both the Boer War and the Natal Rebellion of 1906. A bright young man and a fine athlete, Pat early on became deeply interested in aviation, and applied to join the South African air force when he turned eighteen. Rejected for "lack of flying"—only a true bureaucrat could think of that one—he paid for private lessons.

When the Royal Air Force began its expansion in the mid-1930s, another avenue opened for Pattle, and he flew to England at his own expense, went through the qualification process, and was offered a commission; he returned to South Africa and then reversed course for England as an immigrant. Pattle went through flight school smoothly, scoring very high in his examinations and rated as "exceptional" at the end of his schooling. He became a pilot officer in the summer of 1937.

He had trained on the Gloster Gauntlet, an obsolescent biplane fighter, until he was assigned to the Gauntlet's successor, the Gloster Gladiator. The Gladiator was itself obsolescent by this time, but remained in service until enough Hurricanes and Spitfires were delivered. It was a tough, agile, little biplane, capable of about 250 miles per hour at top speed, and it carried four rifle-caliber machine guns. It had an enclosed cockpit, too, as the Gauntlet did not. In terms of speed, climb, and fire-power, the Spitfires and Hurricanes outclassed the little biplane, but in

Pattle's hands the Gladiator became a classic fighter. He was a pilot of great natural ability, and like Ball and Mannock and other World War I aces, he constantly practiced his shooting. Also like both of them, Pattle tried to hold his fire until the range was virtually point-blank.

In the summer of 1940, Pattle saw his first action, a fight against Italian Breda light bombers and Fiat CR.42 biplane fighters. Pattle got one of each, but was shot down by a second Fiat, landing far enough away in the desert that it took him a day to find his way to a patrol of the 11th Hussars, who took him home. Pattle's pride was hurt—to be shot down by the Italians? And he vowed that his wandering in the desert would not be repeated either; he flew to Alexandria and bought a compass, which flew with him ever after.

On August 8 Pattle's squadron jumped a larger number of Fiats and shot down several without loss. Pattle got two of them. Then on September 6 the Italians invaded Egypt, but to Pattle's disgust his squadron's role was limited to ground support; Pattle's orders prohibited aerial combat "unless attacked," a recipe for frustration at best and disaster.

Then, in November, the squadron moved to help the minuscule Greek air force fight off the Italian invasion pouring down from the north. In a series of close-in dogfights, Pattle and his boys repeatedly took on Italian fighters and bombers, always emerging as victors. By February 9, 1941, he had run his string of victories to fifteen; two days later he received the Distinguished Flying Cross.

All his victories to date had been in the aging Gladiator, but that was about to change. The squadron was re-equipped with eight-gun Hurricanes, and Pattle quickly ran his score to twenty-one. He was part of the RAF's biggest Greek success on February 28, when 80 Squadron claimed twenty-seven kills in a single battle, when they were attacked while escorting Blenheim bombers. The Italian air force said its loss was really only seven aircraft and claimed it had shot down not only six Gladiators but one Spitfire. The last claim was highly unlikely, since at the time, there were no Spitfires even in the theater, only one Gladiator failed to return, and two Blenheims had to crash-land . . . but made it home.

In early March Pattle shot down three more Fiat fighters, but the day was badly marred by the disappearance of his wingman, Australian ace

Nigel Cullen. Cullen, a husky officer nicknamed "Ape," was 100 percent Aussie, even though he had been living in London; he had fought against the Spanish Fascists in the International Brigade, until he was badly wounded in the stomach. He was an able motorcycle racer, and had run at prestigious Brooklands. The squadron later learned that he had been shot down and killed. He would be missed.

Pattle carried on. Now the premier scorer among Allied pilots, he had three times claimed five victories in a single day, and on the 19th of April, 1941, he was able to claim six. But Pattle the dedicated warrior was perhaps too demanding of himself . . . for the very next day, after leading several patrols, he took off yet again, this time against orders, flying when he shouldn't have with a high fever turning into influenza.

A German maximum effort, something around one hundred bombers with fighter escort, was inbound for Athens, and there were only some fifteen Hurricanes to stop them. Pattle got up from the couch where he had lain shivering under blankets, ran for his airplane through a German strafing attack, and got into the air to fight off the Germans . . . but this time he didn't come home.

He was last seen destroying a German fighter that had just shot down Irish ace Timber Woods, and then in a dogfight with at least two more German fighters. He shot down a second German, but after that there was nothing heard of him, only a report from one of his pilots who saw "a lone Hurricane" headed for the sea with its pilot crumpled in the cockpit and its engine beginning to burn.

The usual questions are asked about Pattle's true score of victories, as they are about those of most other famous pilots. He claimed fifty-one victories, and he certainly had at least forty. Men of his squadron thought the actual total was closer to sixty. Perhaps the highest compliment came from author Roald Dahl, who served in Greece with Pattle; as Dahl put it, Pattle was quite simply: "The Second World War's greatest flying ace."

CHAPTER TWENTY-FIVE

The Cream of the Crop

David McCampbell (US)

HE SCORED THE HIGHEST NUMBER OF KILLS OF ANY NAVY OR MARINE pilot—and the third highest of any American in World War II. Yet his aerial accomplishments were largely overshadowed by the dramatic battles he fought in.

McCampbell was born in January 1910 in Bessemer, Alabama, a coke- and iron-manufacturing town about eighteen miles south of Birmingham. He had no middle name or initial, but he did have a fascination with aviation. That began when his grandfather bought a surplus Army biplane in 1920. By then McCampbell's father had moved the family to West Palm Beach, Florida, where he established a branch of his Bessemer furniture company. McCampbell graduated from the Staunton Military Academy in Virginia at age eighteen. While there he lettered in swimming and diving.

McCampbell began college at Georgia Tech majoring in engineering, but the family furniture businesses failed that year. Decades later McCampbell told an interviewer that he sought appointment to the US Naval Academy in 1929 to relieve his family of paying college tuition they couldn't afford. He became an intercollegiate diving champion, but like far too many young graduates of that era, he immediately received an honorable discharge upon graduation in 1933 because of the Depression. Despite this he was commissioned in the US Naval Reserve that June and went on active duty the next year.

McCampbell became a gunnery observer officer aboard the USS *Portland* in July 1936 responsible for targeting gunfire. He personally steered the ship under the Golden Gate Bridge during the celebration when it officially opened May 27, 1937. Later the *Portland* participated in the decisive 1944 Battle of Surigao Strait and accepted Japanese surrender of the Caroline Islands.

The next month McCampbell began flight school at the Naval Air Station, Pensacola, Florida, becoming first in the class that graduated in April 1938. And as a consequence of that distinction, he was the first in his class to fly solo. His first assignment aboard the aircraft carrier USS *Ranger* led to a May 1940 assignment on the carrier USS *Wasp* serving as landing signal officer, responsible for control of aircraft approaching for landing.

The *Wasp* was at Grassy (now Jamaica) Bay, Long Island, when the Japanese struck Pearl Harbor. Late the next month she sailed for the British Isles under the command of Rear Admiral John W. Wilcox Jr. Along the way Wilcox was swept overboard from his flagship, the USS *Washington*, and drowned.

The following April, Campbell participated in Operations Calendar and Bowery, delivering Spitfires to beleaguered British forces at Malta, prompting a telegram from Winston Churchill asking, "Who said a wasp couldn't sting twice!"

Refitted and equipped with new Avenger torpedo-bombers and Dauntless dive-bombers, the *Wasp* was Pacific bound, for service at Guadalcanal, the Solomons, and elsewhere. McCampbell and the rest of the deck crew landed eleven aircraft that afternoon just before three Japanese torpedoes struck the *Wasp* in rapid succession on September 12 at 2:45 p.m. One surfaced and hit the ship slightly above the waterline. Thirty-five minutes later the *Wasp* was abandoned.

This course of events shouldn't have been surprising. Although she was the first US aircraft carrier to be fitted with a deck-edge elevator, the *Wasp* had little armor, very modest speed capability, and little protection around her boilers and aviation fuel storage tanks. These known vulnerabilities prompted one historian to describe her as doomed from the very beginning to a blazing demise.

Champion diver that he was, McCampbell thought about doing a half-somersault from the flight deck as the *Wasp* sank, but then just jumped in order to minimize contact with debris and other survivors. He recalled later being in the water over three hours before being rescued. One hundred ninety-three men died and more than three hundred were wounded.

Stateside again, he trained landing signal officers until August 1943, when he stepped up to take the most important assignments of his life. First he organized Fighter Squadron 15 (VF-15) in early September 1943. Four months later he became commander of Air Group 15 aboard the USS *Essex* in charge of fighters, bombers, and dive-bombers. By then the *Essex* crew he had joined was well seasoned, with prior experience in the Marianas Islands, Tinian, and Guam.

His first two personal air kills came June 11 and June 13. Six days later he led the "Fabled Fifteen" (as his group was later known) into the First Battle of the Philippine Sea, which became known as the "Great Marianas Turkey Shoot." That day the Fifteen took on some eighty Japanese aircraft. McCampbell destroyed at least seven himself.

The Japanese had initiated the battle in a vain effort to hold the Marianas Islands. Some 750 Japanese army and navy planes faced off against 956 carrier-based US Navy and Marine pilots who had three distinct advantages: extensive prior combat experience; comprehensive radar support; and early, massive reconnaissance in which the Navy used both surface and air patrols to monitor Japanese movements from the very beginning of the engagement.

That Thursday June 19 found Commander McCampbell and the formation he led intercepting some one hundred Japanese planes coming to attack the *Essex*. He ordered four pilots to stay at twenty-five thousand feet and began an attack on enemy dive-bombers four thousand feet below them. McCampbell's first target exploded, but he had to climb up and out of the withering machine gun fire; seconds later he took out another dive-bomber and yet another before spotting the Japanese flight leader.

McCampbell missed the leader on his first pass, but got the Japanese wingman. All six of his guns jammed during a second try for the leader. He got the starboard (right) half of his firepower working again, continued chasing the leader, and finally knocked him out even as the force of the working guns pushed the plane to the port (left) side, causing McCampbell to constantly correct his course and direction. He now had just enough ammunition to down one more plane before seeing a bomb strike the USS *South Dakota* in the waters beneath him, killing or wounding fifty seamen as he returned to the *Essex*.

McCampbell was in the air again at 2:25 leading eleven other pilots toward Guam to attack the Japanese airfield there. The attack began from twenty-four thousand feet. He quickly took out another enemy plane, just before two more began chasing Ens. R. L. Nall, his wingman that day. McCampbell shot down one of the pursuers and forced the other to make an emergency landing at Japanese-held Orote Field. Minutes later he provided cover for two American seaplanes picking up downed American flyers in the water before returning to the *Essex* for the day.

But much more action was ahead. As part of Third Fleet Task Force, the *Essex* supported the October 20 invasion of the Philippines and the ensuing naval battle, which at least one Japanese admiral thought at the time would decide the war. The Second Battle of the Philippine Sea, later renamed the Battle of Leyte Gulf, was the largest naval battle of World War II, arguably the largest in history, and marked the beginning of organized Japanese *kamikaze* attacks.

The Allies initiated the action to deprive the Japanese of critical petroleum resources and succeeded in doing so. Most of the heavy Japanese ships that survived the battle remained harbored for the duration of the war.

Leyte Gulf began for McCampbell in the early hours of October 24 when an orderly woke him to report that a dawn launch was planned and McCampbell would be part of it. Instead, he led the second strike that had been scheduled for nine, but launched early after part of the Japanese fleet was spotted on the far distant western horizon.

And launching early meant an emergency takeoff with his main fuel tanks only half full, just after a third Japanese naval force appeared on the ship radar as an expected Japanese counterattack began. The task force chief of staff had specifically ordered McCampbell to sit this one out, but later all fighter pilots were ordered aloft on the ship loudspeakers. He disobeyed the earlier direct order, personally leading the last seven fighter pilots on the *Essex* into the fray.

His wingman, Ens. Roy Warrick Rushing, eleven years younger than McCampbell, had been born in Macon, Missouri, 179 miles northwest of St. Louis, but by the time the war began had settled in McGehee, Arkansas, some 117 miles northwest of Vicksburg, Mississippi. His father, Aubrey L. Rushing, had served as an artillery sergeant during World War I.

During the October 24 attack, Roy Rushing stayed up with McCampbell, but the other five pilots were behind and below them as they closed on the enemy, some twenty-two miles away. McCampbell spotted sixty or more Japanese planes. The bombers were flying at about eighteen thousand feet, with the fighters some four thousand feet above them as McCampbell and Rushing pushed their Hellcats even higher for an attack.

McCampbell ordered the other five planes in his group to go in low for the bombers and then called back to the *Essex* for reinforcements, even as he began the attack on the Japanese fighters now configured in three V formations. He aimed at the most vulnerable spot on any Japanese Zeke, the military nickname for the Zero.

And that vulnerable target was the "wing root," the very place where wing met fuselage; McCampbell watched the first target spiral out of control and flamed a second. He watched in frustration as the rest of the now-alerted Japanese fighters began to fly a "Lufbery circle." In that tactic, named for the World War I ace who popularized it, fighters under attack formed into a large circle to minimize blind spots and maximize their fire against hostile planes. While he waited for a possible opening, McCampbell scored hits on two Japanese fighters, but neither fell from the sky. Just as one of the five pilots who had attacked bombers at lower altitudes now joined McCampbell, the Japanese fighters broke and set course for their airfield on Luzon, suggesting that they may have been as low on fuel as he was.

And so McCampbell led a trio of Hellcats closing in on the Japanese fighters. Within minutes he destroyed a straggler, only to see friendly fire arcing toward him. After some frank radio chatter, McCampbell hit another Japanese fighter, his fourth of the day, followed by another two in quick succession and then number seven.

Now Japanese-held Luzon loomed in the near distance, even as the enemy planes descended to a lower altitude, where enemy spotters could identify and target the Americans. McCampbell was short on fuel and bullets, but picked off yet another straggler just off the coast, his eighth of the day. He rolled over and downed number nine with the last of his ammunition. His fuel tanks held all of forty-five gallons for the one-hundred-mile trip back to the *Essex*. Worse yet, radio contact was spotty at best. As they approached USS *Hornet*, a sister carrier, unidentified bursts from five-inch guns and other Hellcats rose to attack McCampbell and his group, causing them to use more fuel in evasive maneuvers to escape the friendly fire.

He was down to twenty-five gallons as he approached the *Essex*, whose flight deck was stacked with other planes. Rushing and McCampbell were waved off; they tried for the *Lexington* some one thousand yards away, but once again there was no room at the inn.

USS *Langley* was also covered with planes, but launched nine of them to make room. After McCampbell and Rushing landed, McCampbell's engine stopped for want of fuel, but at least he had six bullets to spare. Task Force chief of staff Adm. Charles R. Brown sent him directly to Rear Admiral Frederick Sherman, the Task Force commander and the very man who ordered him to stand down. McCampbell reminded Sherman about the "scramble all fighters" order blasted on the horn. Sherman admonished him to not let that happen again but let him go.

That evening the *Musashi*, then one of Japan's two greatest battleships, hammered by nineteen torpedoes and seventeen bombs, rolled over and sank.

McCampbell racked up another four kills that November, bringing his grand total to thirty-four, although Rear Admiral Sherman was less impressed with his organizational skills than McCampbell's fighting acumen. He returned stateside in January 1945 to receive the Medal of Honor personally from President Roosevelt in the White House. That March, McCampbell became chief of staff to the commander of fleet air at Norfolk, Virginia, and served in several other capacities before commanding the aircraft carrier USS *Bon Homme Richard*.

He served on the staff of the Joint Chiefs of Staff at the Pentagon before he retired from the Navy. The measure of the man is best summed up by the citation for his Congressional Medal of Honor:

> *For conspicuous gallantry and intrepidity at the risk of his life above and beyond the call of duty as commander Group 15, during combat against enemy Japanese aerial forces in the First and Second Battles of the Philippine Sea. An inspiring leader, fighting boldly in the face of terrific odds, Commander McCampbell led his fighter planes against a force of eighty Japanese carrier-based aircraft bearing down on our Fleet on June 19, 1944. Striking fiercely in valiant defense of our surface force, he personally destroyed seven hostile planes during this single engagement in which the outnumbering attack force was utterly routed and virtually annihilated. During a major Fleet engagement with the enemy on October 24, Commander McCampbell, assisted by but one plane, intercepted and daringly attacked a formation of sixty hostile land-based craft approaching our forces. Fighting desperately but with superb skill against such overwhelming airpower, he shot down nine Japanese planes and, completely disorganizing the enemy group, forced the remainder to abandon the attack before a single aircraft could reach the Fleet. His great personal valor and indomitable spirit of aggression under extremely perilous combat conditions reflect the highest credit upon Commander McCampbell and the United States Naval Service.*

Little known to the public then or now, David McCampbell was the only American who ever became "ace in a day" twice. His Air Group 15 destroyed 315 enemy planes in the air, another 348 on the ground, and sank three hundred thousand tons of enemy shipping, more than any other air group in the Pacific. "Indomitable spirit" indeed!

CHAPTER TWENTY-SIX

Young Finucane of the Shamrock

Paddy Finucane (RAF)

HE WAS A CHILD OF THE IRISH TROUBLES, NEARLY KILLED AS AN INFANT in the arms of his English immigrant mother. They were caught in the crossfire between the Black and Tans and the IRA on the outskirts of Dublin at Rathmines, the very place where Cromwell's forces were defeated in 1649. Yet Brendan Eamonn Fergus "Paddy" Finucane had his eye on the sky at a very young age; he became a British idol and the scourge of the Luftwaffe.

Finucane was Dublin-born in 1920. His father was in the IRA at the very time Brendan's grandfather, Charles Finucane, served England in the King's Own Scottish Borderers, a situation not as unusual as one might think.

At age twelve Brendan and his younger brother, Raymond, took a ten-minute flight during an air show southwest of Dublin. After his 1936 graduation from a Christian Brothers school in Dublin, he moved to the London suburbs, took an office job in the West End, but got his father's blessing the next year to join the Royal Air Force for a Short Service Commission (SSC) as a flying school cadet. Brendan applied in 1938 the day he met the minimum age requirement. But his earliest training days hardly portended the fighter pilot he was to become.

Finucane's greatest challenge was landing. Letters home told of his third landing mishap destroying the landing gear of his Tiger Moth biplane. In those days his flying name became Paddy, although friends and family always called him Brendan or "Bren."

He nearly stalled his plane during his first solo flight September 2, but landed quite nicely at Sywell near Northampton in the English Midlands. And then Finucane was off to Montrose in the eastern highlands of Scotland with hopes of besting the "average" assessments he'd received so far in flight school.

The challenge was to improve during one hundred hours of flight crammed into an eight-month course attended by some forty-five student pilots. And he had to land the Hawker Hart, a two-seater biplane. One flying student recalled the Hart as magnificent and exciting, but to land the thing, one had to turn off the engine and glide in. One of Finucane's instructors at Montrose posed his landing problem succinctly, recalling that the ground was never quite where Paddy thought it was.

Photographs of those early days reveal a photogenic, narrow-faced, chisel-chinned dark Irishman. Finucane was comfortable in his own skin and the military clothes around it. One would never know that he was facing being washed out of flight school. The squadron leader gave him a formal letter saying his performance was under review as he left for home on leave in March 1939; back in training he began flying a new airplane, the Hawker Fury, a fighter counterpart to the Hawker Hart Finucane had flown earlier.

He left Montrose an average flying student whose two recent crashes were being evaluated. Two weeks after World War II began for Britain in early September 1939, Finucane was reinstated. But instead of going into action, he was consigned to transport duty for ground staff. Finucane itched to get in the action but continued ferrying duty until late June 1940, when, at last, he was sent to an airfield near Chester for Spitfire training, the prelude to becoming a fighter pilot.

His first Spitfire landing was chancy, to say the least, too fast and too high, forcing Finucane to drop quickly at the last minute, where he was almost out of runway. Altogether Finucane logged about twenty-two hours on his new plane before beginning his first assignment with a fighter squadron in mid-July, just as the Battle of Britain began.

The squadron star was Bill "Gunner" Franklin, a scruffy former airplane mechanic from East London who had shot down ten enemy aircraft since late May, not to mention two shared kills. Finucane's first scramble in late July promptly ended when fumes from the plane's de-icing system filled the cockpit, forcing him to crash-land at Manston Field, even as Franklin splashed a Messerschmitt Bf 109 in the Channel.

His time came on August 12, some ten miles out over the Channel near the North Foreland on the Kent Coast. Finucane shook off a 109 while protecting a buddy, then flew to twenty thousand feet looking for prospects. He nuzzled in behind a German formation of twelve, blasted one from fifty feet away, and returned to base. At 11:45 a.m., a quick celebration began when another pilot confirmed the kill.

But shortly after he landed, German planes ruined the party by beginning bomb runs and strafing attacks at Manston Field. One pilot saw the dust and smoke rising where the bombs had fallen, even as he started his own rapid ascent into the air. Another airman left behind wondered where his ground crew had gone until he saw wings emblazoned with iron crosses flashing just above him. Even then Finucane was chasing a Messerschmitt above the town of Margate into the clouds.

Within seconds Finucane encountered another one; he later claimed that he damaged the first and probably destroyed the second plane he'd been chasing. Finucane scored again the next day near Dover. These early Battle of Britain scores earned him a September 3 promotion from pilot officer to flying officer, the journeyman rank. By then the squadron had moved to Turnhouse near Edinborough, where they practiced and learned new tactics from Polish pilot Boleslaw "Ski" Drobinski.

Several moves later the squadron billeted near Chichester in late November, then went thirty miles to the west, to Southampton, which had been badly battered by German bombers.

Finucane caught another German bird on January 4, 1941, near Selsey Bill in Sussex, but it did not go quietly. The enemy pilot had spotted four 65 Squadron Spitfires and run for France, but Finucane sent him into the Channel. And that was just before lunch. Following the midday meal he seriously damaged a Junkers Ju 88 attack bomber whose rear gunner took out Finucane's hydraulic system. According to one account, the Ju 88 crashed near Cherbourg, but Finucane had to do a belly landing.

A month and a day later, 65 Squadron flew to St. Omer on an early afternoon sweep, giving Finucane an opportunity to slide in behind a 109, which he machine-gunned from 250 yards, sending the German into some snow-covered trees to explode.

That April he became a flight lieutenant and was placed in command of A Flight, 452 Squadron, consisting mainly of Royal Australian Air Force flyers. But before departure he shot down a 109 between Calais and Dover. His Distinguished Flying Cross arrived later that month.

Early the next month Finucane made quite an impression on the 452 Squadron commander Roy Dutton over Yorkshire by chopping most of the tail off of Dutton's Spitfire. Dutton crash-landed, but while he was hospitalized Finucane temporarily took command of the entire squadron. This was not the only mishap in the A Flight. After a few more non-lethal accidents, someone from another squadron sketched some door signage calling them "Bend 'Em Brendan and his Demolition Squad." Finucane left the sign on full display.

He got a new Spitfire on May 21; with help from a peacetime lithographer, his ground crew painted a green shamrock on his fuselage. Finucane filled the next eleven days with training and more training. The 452 was ready for flight operations on June 2, 1941, eight days before Dutton's replacement arrived. And on July 11, 452 Squadron joined "the Circus," an air offensive designed by air vice-marshal Trafford Leigh-Mallory the preceding February. His objective: to force battle upon German fighters to divert them from attacking Allied bombers.

The first 452 Circus operation (officially Circus 44), conducted on July 11, used a Blenheim bomber as a decoy, flying via Dunkirk into France. They were near Lille by three, when Finucane spotted eight German fighters coming down at them through ack-ack fire. He followed the leader down, gave the 109 a three-second burst from 150 yards, and watched the pilot bail out.

Another mission to St. Omer on August 3 brought five 109s coming after the 452 at fourteen thousand feet. Finucane followed one of them into a cloud, gave him a long burst as they emerged, watched the plane go down in flames, and then shot down another several minutes later. Thirteen days later he machine-gunned another 109 into an all-but-certain death drop near Gravelines before lunch; he flew again that evening, shot down another 109, and survived a near collision to fly another day.

On August 21 Finucane added two more 109s during Circus 81, becoming one of three British flyers to add a bar to his DFC the next day, signifying that he had earned a second such award; Finucane's official score for August 1941 was nine of the twenty-two 452 Squadron claimed to destroy. A competing squadron officially asked higher authorities to look into whether the 452 flyers had exaggerated their statistics. After the ensuing investigation the inquiring flyers lost two of their own August kills while the 452 Squadron statistics were not reduced at all.

September 5 brought unexpected fame for Finucane. The British Air Ministry public relations department now considered him a solid replacement for Douglas Bader, the double amputee who had gone missing in his Spitfire on August 9 and was captured. The *Daily Herald* declared Finucane Bader's natural successor, reporting that he had destroyed at least fifteen German fighters, proclaiming that 452 Squadron had recently tackled one hundred Messerschmitts, holding off thirty by itself for twenty-five minutes.

Of course, the publicity blitz wasn't hurt at all by Finucane's highly photogenic appearance; he became as famous in Australia as in Britain. His official score jumped in September, and Finucane received a second DFC bar as well. But two squadron members were killed in training exercises, and two more in combat September 18.

"Show on, Chaps," someone from 11 Group headquarters yelled to Finucane on the telephone the morning of September 20 as Spitfire engines fired up in the background. Circus 100B was about to begin; the 452 Squadron target: Abbeville.

Just northwest of the target, a dozen Messerschmitts crossed from left to right in front of Finucane. He missed the first target in his sights, then a second 109, but the third enemy pilot wasn't so lucky.

Three 452 Squadron pilots went down about then, as Finucane and Sgt. Keith Chisholm climbed to ten thousand feet to see how much of the squadron was left; nobody was home, but a 109 flew by Finucane, either out of ammunition or tired of fighting. Finucane wasn't tired at all. He closed from behind, shot at the German wing root and engine, and then followed the German down to fifteen hundred feet, where flames erupted, then bagged one more on the way home. Finucane and Chisholm were greeted by fellow pilots and photographers eager for news.

Finucane increased his number by two the next afternoon flying with Circus 101 toward a power station at Gosnay, in northern France. The Flying Shamrock was credited with his twentieth (reported as twenty-first) kill on October 2 during a sweep from Mardyck to Boulogne four-teen days before his twenty-first birthday. Now out of ammunition, he only survived because he barrel-rolled to ditch the 109s chasing him. During inclement weather in the days that followed, there was time for farewells to several squadron members moving on to other assignments, and parties in the West End of London, where Finucane spent time with Jean Woolford. Quite soon they began discussing marriage.

The 452 Squadron learned on October 11 that it had received the Distinguished Service Order. But Circus 107 was scheduled for noon the next day. And Alex Roberts, who had been shot down back in July, had just made his way back from behind enemy lines to cheer them on. He'd turned up on the evening of October 10, of all places at the 452 Squadron's favorite hangout, Oddeninno's Restaurant, in London's West End; at first no one knew who he was. In fact, his baggy trousers were so dirty the doorman kept Roberts outside until Finucane recognized him.

Their target the morning of Sunday, October 12, was Boulogne again, but the order of battle was more robust, nineteen Spitfire squadrons in all. The Blenheim bombers struck the Boulogne docks without incident, but then, from out of nowhere, the Messerschmitt fighters appeared out of the clouds. 452 Squadron, consisting of some twelve planes, was overwhelmed by fifty German fighters. Finucane picked one of the twenty that appeared in his windscreen, poured cannon and machine gun fire into the enemy engine, cockpit, and tail, followed the 109 down to ten thousand feet, and watched it burst into flames. But his wingman, Sergeant Chisholm, was shot down. He parachuted from his stricken

Spitfire, was sent to Stalag 8b in Silesia, and joined the renowned British ace Douglas Bader there.

That Monday Finucane scored two more 109s and got back in time for the news to be distributed by the air ministry before midnight. But another kind of danger awaited Finucane in the darkened streets of Croydon the next evening. After being over-served at the Greyhound Pub, he bounded over the town hall parapet and took an eighteen-foot fall, fracturing his right heel bone. An extra pint of Guinness had done what dozens of Messerschmitts had failed to do. "Finucane of the Shamrock," as some German pilots called him, was out of action.

While in the hospital, his brother, Raymond, reminded him that at a fair back in Dublin a palm reader told Brendan that he would die at twenty-one, but Brendan was far more concerned about being laid up several months healing. At another hospital, this in Buckinghamshire, he walked to Sunday mass in mid-November, although his foot was still in a cast, then was formally invested with his Distinguished Flying Cross by the king on November 24. He returned to service at Kenley in late November, and was appointed commander of the 602 Squadron on January 25 by station commander Victor Beamish, a fellow Irishman.

Their new field at Redhill, a Surrey suburb south of London, featured a red Victorian mansion converted to become the officer's dining hall. During evening drinks at Chequers, their new pub near Crawley, the 602 pilots fretted about the winter weather that kept them grounded.

All that changed at about 11:00 the morning of February 13, when 602 Squadron was ordered into the air as part of Operation Fuller, an attack on German battleships *Scharnhorst* and *Gneisenau* and heavy cruiser *Prinz Eugen*. This was the long-awaited German attempt—code-named *Cerberus*—to break out the heavy ships from the British blockade that had bottled them helplessly in French Channel ports.

845 Squadron, flying six obsolete Swordfish torpedo bombers, rose to meet the German breakout the morning of February 12, expecting to rendezvous with five Spitfire squadrons, but could finally find but one squadron. The old biplanes were all lost; only five crew members survived. Next day, when 602 was put on standby, the rendezvous with more bombardment aircraft misfired again. Finucane's pilots finally attacked

two armed merchantmen and some other vessels. The big game, the battleships, got away to shelter in home waters, although both struck British mines during their flight.

Gneisenau's damage was more than initially thought, and she was sent to dry dock in Kiel. There, only about two weeks after the successful "dash," the RAF hit her with two very heavy bombs. She was a useless hulk for the rest of the war.

Finucane testified in the board of inquiry that followed the failure to prevent the Channel breakout. The board correctly concluded that the embarrassing failure was the result of inadequate reconnaissance.

The next morning he was off on another "rhubarb," a sort of freelance raid to beat up on anything German. This one was aimed at the Dunkirk area, and here his men saw a new airplane bearing black crosses. It was the Focke-Wulf Fw190, which outperformed the Spitfire models Finucane and his men were flying. Pilot Dick Lewis, flying wing to Finucane, knocked down a 190; all Finucane got was a bullet in the leg and a few days in the hospital.

On Friday, March 13, he was back bringing bad luck to the Luftwaffe again. Covering a bombing mission over northern France, he got another 190, and shared a second with another pilot. Next day he shared a Ju 88 with two other fighter pilots. Then came St. Patrick's Day, on which he helped another pilot celebrate a new assignment, something different for the man his pilots remember as a bit of a loner, but a daring leader who demanded and got results.

He laid on another rhubarb for March 25, with the blessing of Group Captain Beamish, and followed up with an "official" mission, "Circus 116A" or "Ramrod 17," a bombing visit to the docks at Le Havre, escorting two dozen Douglas A-20 Bostons. It was a long run in, and the Germans were waiting. Finucane got one with a remarkable cannon shot at about five hundred yards, and the Bostons left the targeted docks a ruin under a cloud of reddish-brown smoke.

A "no bombers" run followed on March 28, 1942, said to be the biggest German-British dogfight since the Battle of Britain. Group Captain Beamish did not get home that day, but Finucane got two 109s to run his score to 29.5. In April he hit and damaged several Focke-Wulf Fw190s, but with no solid confirmation that any of them had crashed. The high spot of the month was his engagement to Jean Woolford.

The next run was escorting Bostons to strike the Boulogne docks, and when the German defenders came up, Finucane shot one of them down. He scored a "damaged" on June 8, but then it was time to take over his new duties as the commander of the Hornchurch Wing. He had risen to the top quickly, taking command of a wing after only about a year's service.

He led practice sweeps during the last ten days of June, and then went to more escort runs with British bombers. The last of these was a strike at an infantry post at Etades, in northern France. Pouring over maps of the objective before the raid, Finucane had reserved the German officers' mess as his personal target.

But on the way to Etades with his men, crossing German beach defenses at Le Touquet, ground fire tore into his radiator. He stayed in the air, but it quickly became obvious to him that he could not continue. Passing command to one of his men, he turned sharply back toward England. He didn't make it.

He flew about ten miles toward safety, and then had to try to ditch. Nobody saw the last minutes of Finucane and his Spitfire. The sea is said to have been rough that day and the aircraft was not built to float. He might have had a few seconds to get out of the fighter before she sank, maybe even less. In any case, Paddy Finucane, not quite twenty-two years old, was gone forever.

CHAPTER TWENTY-SEVEN

Adlertag

Hermann Goering, marshal of Germany's much-touted air force, had made a solemn promise to *der Fuhrer* that an all-out air offensive against England would wipe out the RAF's Fighter Command in a matter of weeks, perhaps even days. Then the way would be clear for Operation Sea Lion, the invasion of the British Isles. Once the Luftwaffe had destroyed Fighter Command, German aircraft could not only bomb tactical targets at will, but keep the Royal Navy from interfering with the army's landing and resupply. Hitler bought his fat subordinate's assurance, and the Luftwaffe launched its offensive—called *Adlerangriff*—Eagle Attack—on the 13th of August, 1940, a beautiful summer's day. The Germans called it *Adlertag*, Eagle Day.

Der Dicke (The Fat Man)'s confident boast would come back to haunt him, but the *Blitzkrieg* had been a great success thus far, and no one could be sure that "the few" could stand up to Hitler's sophisticated fighting forces.

The RAF fighter squadrons were scattered on fields along the Channel coast, mostly grass strips. Others were concentrated north and east of London, but still within reach of any invasion beach along the crucial stretch of coast from Dover west to Southampton. The British had an ace in the hole as well: the radar stations scattered along the south coast, supplemented by a small army of civilian volunteer aircraft spotters, the Royal Observer Corps. The radar system was called RDF—radio direction-finding—by the British; the title was sufficiently non-specific by design, so as not to emphasize the importance of it as a target.

Fighter Command's nerve center was at RAF Bentley Priory, a stately building on the edge of London, dating from 1766. The chief of Fighter Command, Air Chief Marshal Hugh "Stuffy" Dowding, commanded from the building, which housed the operations room. It was staffed by WAAFs—Women's Auxiliary Air Force service women—who received information about German activity by telephone from the RDF stations, the Royal Observer Corps, "Y Service" radio monitoring of German transmissions, and Bletchley Park, the top-secret center that read Germany's secret mail from Ultra.

This information was plotted on a large table-grid, each German threat indicated by a marker, pushed over the table by a WAAF with a magnetized rake. Dowding and his officers could see at a glance the strength, altitude, and direction of each threat; the color of the marker told them how current the information was. The same information was sent to each fighter group, which was also receiving information from its airstrips and the observer corps. Fighter Command's reaction to German threats was typically swift and accurate.

The Luftwaffe had suffered substantial casualties that spring during the fighting over France, hence the delay in launching Eagle Day. Preliminaries began with several days of attacks on British coastal shipping, and by the 12th of August, the Germans were striking hard at several radar stations and fighter airstrips. The damage at some places was heavy, especially at Ventnor radar station, but by the morning of the 12th, all the radar sets were up and running including Ventnor, and the scattered fighter stations were operational. If all your enemy's bombs do is make holes in grassy pastures, the damage is repairable quite quickly; damage to hangars and other buildings doesn't stop flying missions ("ops" in RAF lingo) either as long as you can refuel and rearm between flights. The British could; the Germans could not, another factor that loomed larger and larger as the long summer went on. The German aircraft could not stay in the air above England as long as the RAF could. And British pilots with disabled aircraft could make emergency landings or bale out over friendly country and fly again; a German pilot had to choose between captivity and the chance of going down in the Channel short of home.

But the Germans clearly felt their early raids had severely hurt Fighter Command, and so on the 12th the great Eagle Day offensive began, hurling hundreds of twin-engined bombers, fighters, and Junkers Ju 87 Stuka dive-bombers at England. German tactics were less than subtle . . . or effective. The Luftwaffe flew some initial sweeps ahead of the bombers, the notion being to get the RAF to commit early, leaving a clear path for the bombers.

Instead, the tactic only helped alert the defense. One Stuka squadron attacked with nine aircraft; only three flew back across the Channel, for the fearsome dive-bomber had more serious opposition over England than it had ever faced above the Continent. Some German attacks struck the wrong target, bomber airfields instead of fighter strips; one Ju 87 attack had to drop its bombs randomly. Another managed to wipe out both a furniture warehouse and a bicycle plant. The only really serious damage and casualties were inflicted at RAF Station Detling, where several Blenheim bombers were destroyed on the ground and the operations staff took heavy casualties. But the Detling station housed light bombers, so the raid had not the slightest effect on Fighter Command.

Other German attacks were similar failures, although they were accompanied by a series of wild claims about RAF losses. The raid on RAF Farnborough, for example, developed into a monster dogfight, in the wake of which the Luftwaffe claimed it had shot down twenty British planes. Actual losses were one shot down and six damaged; only three pilots were wounded, and nobody was killed.

Radio direction-finding and the alertness of the observers had given the RAF fighters time to scramble ahead of German raids on their fields. A small number of aircraft had been destroyed on the ground, but those losses had no impact on Fighter Command.

That night the raids continued, scattered all across Britain, as far north as Edinborough. British casualties were about one hundred, and the damage was negligible. What casualties the Germans suffered that night remain unknown, although one Luftwaffe man was discovered wandering through the night down in the Somerset countryside. All in all, Adlertag was a colossal flop.

German intelligence had failed to provide the air force with adequate hard information; some RAF stations were attacked repeatedly even though they had no connection with Fighter Command. By contrast, with few exceptions Dowding's people and system performed as they were meant to, and the Spitfires and Hurricanes did the rest, ably supported by the WAAF plotters, the observers, the radio interceptors, and the wizards of Bletchley Park.

In round figures Eagle Day had cost the Luftwaffe forty-seven or forty-eight aircraft destroyed plus about forty more damaged. Forty-four pilots had been killed, about the same number were missing, and more were wounded. By comparison, Fighter Command had lost just thirteen fighters in the fight for the sky, plus one on the ground; only three fighter pilots had been killed. Other losses were grievous: Several hundred civilians had been killed or injured and Bomber Command had lost eleven aircraft and two dozen aircrew.

But Britain's vital weapon was Fighter Command that summer, and Dowding's pilots and aircraft not only remained the sharpest of weapons, but had honed their combat skills. They would need their sharp edge to fight off the continuing German attacks, for England and a lot of other nations were depending on them.

It would be a long summer.

CHAPTER TWENTY-EIGHT

Just One More

Gabby Gabreski (US)

He wasn't exactly born to be a fighter pilot. In fact, during his first flying days at South Bend, Indiana, while a pre-med student at Notre Dame, he showed little promise in either pursuit. Yet Francis Stanley "Gabby" Gabreski eventually exceeded the records of such notable air aces as World War I flyer Eddie Rickenbacker and Richard Bong, Gabby's contemporary in the Pacific. And this despite being told on his first flight that he "didn't have the touch of a pilot."

His parents were immigrant Polish who found their way to Oil City, Pennsylvania, and then found each other. Gabby's dad had simplified the family name from Gabryszewski to Gabreski, worked on the railroad and in a foundry, but had to find lighter work due to a debilitating thyroid problem. Eventually he bought a grocery store with borrowed money and made it a success with fourteen-hour days, personal deliveries, and door-to-door sales pitches.

This made Notre Dame a feasible college choice for Gabby's older brother, Ted, and six years later Gabby himself, who, when young bore an uncanny, though big-nosed resemblance to Sean Penn. But Gabby struggled academically, only managing to stay in school thanks to study groups with good scholars in his class. During the winter months he developed an interest in airplanes.

At the beginning of his second year, he found a ride to Bendix Airfield, five miles west of Notre Dame, and plopped down in the makeshift office of flying instructor Homer Stockert. His first plane ride was in a Taylor Craft sporting holes in the doors. When Gabby tried a turn at the controls, he nearly put the small plane into a stall.

Gabby took a few more lessons, and was far from flying solo when he ran out of money and signed up with Army Air Corps recruiters visiting the campus. His parents were disappointed, yet pleased with the news weeks later that their son had been accepted for air cadet training in July 1940. That month gallant flyers in Spitfires and Hurricanes were fighting the Luftwaffe in the skies over Britain. He caught a ride to Pittsburgh, some ninety miles south of Oil City, for his physical, then hitchhiked to East St. Louis, Illinois, for primary flight training.

Parks Air College, a proprietary school established the very year Lindbergh soloed the Atlantic, then trained many Army Air Corps pilots. Ground training was easier for Gabby thanks to Homer Stockert back in South Bend. Flying a PT-17 Stearman biplane was another matter. But the old tightness returned, and the brittle, demanding tone of his instructor, George Myers, made things worse. Yet, after twelve hours flight instructor Myers declared him ready for his first solo flight.

Gabby was good at takeoffs, but his first landing was so bad he had no choice but to power off the runway and back into the air. When he finally did bounce onto the runway and taxied over to Myers, the instructor just shook his head in disgust. He flubbed all of the maneuvers he was supposed to be learning, including the lazy eight, so Myers gave him one last chance in an "elimination flight," which would be conducted by another instructor, Capt. Ray Wassel.

Buoyed by some prayers in the local parish church and encouragement from Wassel, Gabby got by the elimination flight with several lazy eights, a 180-degree turn combined with a steep climb called a chandelle, and a competent last-minute forced landing at an auxiliary field. Wassel diagnosed the problem as a personality conflict between Gabby and Myers. His new instructor, a Mr. Peterson, had a style that echoed Homer Stockert, and Gabby finished that November 1940. He was then off to Gunther Army Air Base near Montgomery, Alabama, for basic flight training.

His first choices had been Kelly and Randolph Fields in Texas, but he was flying the BF 132 trainer, which the students called the Vultee Vibrator. He steadily progressed through maneuvers, instruments, and navigation, but another trainee pilot he remembered only as "Blackie" parachuted out of his plane during an unintended nose dive, had his legs chopped off by the prop, and floated to earth dead.

During advanced training at nearby Maxwell Field, Gabby nearly washed out after passing out for a few seconds in a formation. After Gabby admitted to his commanding officer that he'd solved the problem by taking blood pressure medicine, he was reinstated and sent on his dream assignment to Wheeler Field in Hawaii, adjoining Pearl Harbor. Hawaiian girls placed leis around the new boys' necks in late March 1941, before he started the twenty-five-minute trip to his first assignment.

He saw Kay Cochran for the first time one Sunday morning during mass at Schofield Barracks. Several weeks later on Saturday, December 6, they had a lovers' quarrel at an officers' club dance. The next morning while Gabby shaved, he wondered whether they would make up. And then he heard an explosion. The gray monoplane that lumbered over his barracks seconds later didn't have the right insignia.

Gabby woke up everyone he could, dashed five hundred yards with other pilots to the planes parked in rows ever so convenient for the Japanese, and became one of the few in his fighter group who got into the air that morning. Gabby didn't find any Japanese, but the small group he was flying with was nearly brought down by friendly flak. George Welch, who flew in another group, bagged four confirmed kills that morning.

In the summer of 1942, he met legendary Navy fighter pilot Butch O'Hare, for whom the main Chicago airport is named, and Buzz Wagner, the first Army ace of World War II. Gabby soon proposed that the Army send him to learn fighter tactics from Polish fighter pilots serving in the British 303 Squadron. After all, he spoke Polish fluently. And to his surprise the proposal was accepted.

Gabby arrived in London that October, found nothing but blank stares among those at Eighth Air Force headquarters, but was eventually assigned to ferry duty co-piloting B-24s. While on leave in London, he met several officers of another Polish squadron at the posh Embassy Club on Bond Street of all places. After receiving orders to join them, Gabby flew a Spitfire IX for the first time in January 1943.

And soon thereafter he flew into the winter sky for a circus mission to Le Havre with 315 Squadron from Northolt air station in northwest London. Several uneventful missions later he jumped into his Spitfire the morning of Wednesday, February 3, hoping that this trip to St. Omer, twenty-nine miles southeast of Calais, wouldn't be more of the same.

It wasn't. The Focke-Wulf Fw190s came at them from out of the sun, and just as quickly were gone. Gabby had fired at planes that he didn't really see as anything but dots in his windshield. After two dozen or so uneventful missions with the 315, he joined "Hub" Zemke's 56th Fighter Group, 61st Fighter P-47 Squadron, and moved with them to RAF Halesworth, where he was promoted to major.

The P-47 fighters were larger than his Spitfire, but he soon adjusted to the change. Gabby became commander of B Flight in March and helped move the squadron to Horsham St. Faith, about one hundred miles northeast of London, early the next month. On a May 15 mission to Zanvoort, Holland, he shot at an Fw190 from about four hundred yards away, but the enemy plane escaped. Despite his lack of combat experience, Gabby became commander of the 61st Fighter Squadron on June 9. One year before, he'd still been in flight school.

Gabby's first confirmed air victory didn't come until Tuesday, August 24, near Evreux on the Iton River in northern France. From twenty-seven thousand feet, he spotted some Fw190s and dived, leading his wingman, Frank McCauley, down to attack a group of four. Gabby machine-gunned the leader from about 275 yards, and then watched the German crash. Nine days later he spotted an Fw190 lone wolf below him at twenty-eight thousand feet near St. Germain, a western suburb of Paris, while providing cover for B-17 bombers; Gabby dropped behind the German, pulled the trigger at four hundred yards, and watched the enemy fighter begin a spin that turned into a crash confirmed by another B Flight pilot.

Late that October, 56th Fighter Group commander Hobert "Hub" Zemke of Missoula, Montana, now himself an air ace, began encouraging the press to follow "Zemke's Wolf Pack." He added some color by having his pilots emblazon their P-47 fuselages with then-popular Dogpatch characters created by *Lil Abner* cartoonist Al Capp. Zemke wanted the 56th to have one hundred air victories by November 6.

By November 5 Zemke's goal had been reached, with an assist from Gabby, who, according to his own late-life memoir, reached ace status on November 26, with two kills over northern Germany. November 29 brought him a pair of Messerschmitt Bf 109s over Bremen. Three days later a rear gunner in a Junkers Ju 88 twin-engined light bomber severely damaged Gabby's engine; both Gabby and his squadron mate, Norm Brooks, nursed their P-47s back over the Channel to safety.

During "the Big Week" in mid-February, the 56th destroyed fifty-nine German planes in five missions. On February 20 Gabby exploded two Messerschmitt Bf 110s near Koblenz, while watching the sky fill with burning planes and German parachutes. Two days later he knocked down a Focke-Wulf fighter, just before his first strafing attack ever, taking out a bomber on the ground at St. Anthonis, Holland. That very day his squadron scored its one hundredth air victory. Gabby added two air victories on March 16 above Nancy, France, and yet another pair above Nantes on the 27th, but that day he was nearly killed by debris. Two of his good friends were shot down, but fortunately both men survived the war.

Gabby got another scalp on the 8th of May, and on the 22nd he swooped down on no fewer than sixteen Fw190s that didn't see him coming. Gabby bagged two, and then saw a P-47 go down in flames and another trailing dark smoke, before Gabby took out a third German.

That June was his busiest month of the war, but the action came only days before the calendar page was turned to July. He destroyed two Germans on June 22 during an afternoon mission over northern France. The first was on the edge of a hostile fighter formation, at least until Gabby opened up on one of the Messerschmitts; he was way too close and was nearly struck by the unlucky German's fuselage as the opponent seemed to stop in mid-air. Gabby later remembered escaping debris by only a few yards. He now spotted a second one from the same formation a few thousand feet below him, but during his attack that second plane nearly rammed Gabby before the German crashed.

He was making one last run over the Connatre Airdrome in northeast France and was running low on fuel, when a German aircraft popped out of the clouds ahead of him.

The pilot cruised away, oblivious to his possible fate, but Gabby found four more 109s directly above him, shot at one, but then pursued a third and fired at its vulnerable wing roots until it exploded some three hundred yards away. He returned to base tied for top ace in the Eighth Air Force.

Gabby was on bomber escort duty July 5 with Lanny Lanowski, one of the Polish pilots Gabby had recruited, looking for the kill that would make him America's top ace. He spotted one prospect and yet another before spotting three prospects flying together. He followed the 109s at low altitude through a sharp left turn. One of them slipped out of Gabby's sights after a short burst, but came back into focus just in time to take a second burst from eight machine guns. That was enough for the German, who bailed out just before his 109 hit the ground.

Even as the nationwide publicity about Gabby swelled, he wrote Kay and his parents that he expected to be home in August or September. He didn't have to wait that long.

Gabby was scheduled to leave Boxted Airbase on the morning of July 20, 1944, fully expecting to marry Kay within a week or so. But then, with his luggage already on the airplane, Gabby checked the morning flight schedule and told Jim Carter, one of the last remaining pilots of the 61st Squadron now scheduled to return home with him, that he wanted to fly "just one more."

Gabby was quickly on his 166th mission of the war, protecting B-24 bombers flying to some railroad yards near Frankfurt, Germany. The bombing mission to Russelsheim, some nineteen miles southwest of Frankfurt, was successful, but on the return trip, Gabby saw yet another airfield that needed attention at Bassenheim, some seventy-two miles to the northwest of Russelsheim. They destroyed a Heinkel HE-111 on the ground, but on a second strafing run, Gabby took heavy flak and found himself trying to navigate an escape with engine hydraulic fluid covering his windshield, some three hundred miles from the Channel.

Gabby was on the run five days before being captured, but ended up on his way to Stalag Luft I, a prison camp on the Baltic north of Berlin for an impromptu reunion with his former group commander Hub Zemke, who had been shot down the previous October. "We have been waiting for you a long time," said Hanns Scharff, an intelligence officer who spoke perfect English. Gabreski and Zemke's stay there was mostly boring and uneventful, although toward the end there were days of hunger. The last Monday in April 1945, was a rainy day turned bright when the Russians liberated the camp. By 3:30, although they didn't know it, Adolf Hitler was dead.

Gabby returned to London, but within days was in Wisconsin arranging a June marriage that would eventually produce nine children. After brief experiences as a test pilot and Douglas Aircraft foreign sales representative, he rejoined the Army Air Corps in April 1947, five months before it became the Air Force. He finished college two years later at Columbia University in New York, retired from the military in 1967, and spent most of the next twenty years as a Grumman Aerospace Company executive. He died four months after the 9/11 attacks.

But in mid-June 1951 he went on the first of many Korean War missions, flying the F-86 Sabrejet against the lighter, more maneuverable MiG-15 at the advanced fighter pilot age of thirty-two. His first kill in Korea came on July 5, 1951, exactly seven years to the day from the morning he became America's leading ace in World War II, downing a North Korean (or perhaps Russian) pilot. More individual scores came in early September, another in January 1952, and he shared a third the next month. That April his tally was 5.5, making him the first double ace in American history. The Air Force ordered him to call it quits after one hundred Korea missions and 289 flight operations in two wars. His lifetime record was 34.5 enemy aircraft.

Fifty years later in his memoirs, Gabby recalled his extended visit with Harry Truman in the White House, which followed a ticker tape parade in San Francisco. Quite a thrill, he said, for a Polish kid from Oil City who had almost flunked out of flight school.

Only in America.

CHAPTER TWENTY-NINE

Ace of Aces

Adolf Galland (Germany)

ADOLF GALLAND WAS AN ACE SEVERAL TIMES OVER, A DECENT PERSON, a good officer, a superb and experienced pilot . . . and a very lucky man. For he fought long and hard against first-class opponents, and still managed to survive. In the course of his 705 missions, he shot down 104 of Germany's foes, and all of his victories were scored against the western Allies, far more formidable opponents than the Russian aviators out on the Eastern Front.

Growing up between world wars, Galland's passion for flying in general and military aviation in particular started early, but the Treaty of Versailles banned military aviation in Germany, and Galland learned the basics of flying in the same way thousands of other young Germans did. He flew gliders, and the *Reichswehr* established no fewer than ten gliding schools.

Galland was an excellent pilot, and applied for a place in the commercial flying school sponsored by Lufthansa. Competition for a spot was fierce, and Galland was one of just eighteen men selected for flight training out of about four thousand eager applicants. His early training was in unexciting flying boats, but he soon was invited to join the embryo structure that in time would become the Luftwaffe, and for the first time met *der Dicke*—the Fat Man—Hermann Goering, whom at first Galland thought was a good leader, probably on the basis of his impressive record as a fighter pilot in World War I.

In 1933 Galland and others trained in Italy with the *Regia Aeronautica*, and returned to Germany to fly Junkers tri-motor commercial transports. At the end of the year, he was invited to join the new Luftwaffe, and this meant real airplanes, and a career and a status that most young Germans could only dream about in the tough postwar days.

His new career was not all beer and skittles, however; in fact, it almost ended early for keeps, when a day of acrobatics went bad and he clobbered in, spending the next three days in a coma. Among his other injuries were a fractured skull and a damaged eye, which convinced the doctors that he was no longer fit to fly. A friend sat on their report, however, keeping Galland in the air, until a year later he crashed again, with more injury to the damaged eye, including some imbedded glass fragments. Ordered to have his eye tested, Galland still passed easily however . . . not least because he had memorized in advance the contents of the eye charts, helpfully "acquired" by one of his brothers.

In 1937 he at last went to war, flying ground-attack missions in Spain in support of Francisco Franco's Nationalists. Galland proved to be something of a free spirit, for he flew in a swimsuit, chomping on a cigar, in an airplane decorated with a figure of Mickey Mouse. Honored by the Franco government, he left Spain in 1938, but not before making a number of flights in the Messerschmitt Bf 109. Its fine performance moved him to forsake ground support for fighters.

For a brief time in 1938, he was assigned to the Federal Ministry of Aviation, where his job was recommendations for the future of close air support. He proved himself thoughtful and forward-looking, recommending, among other things, drop tanks to extend aircraft range, combining cannon and machine guns to provide more destructive power, and use of aircraft over the points of the army spearhead, one of the hallmarks of the *Blitzkrieg*.

Just before the invasion of Poland in the fall of 1939, Galland was moved to a close-support squadron and flew eighty-seven missions against Poland in the Henschel Hs 123, a biplane with an open cockpit. By now he was determined to pursue a career as a fighter pilot, and so he obtained a transfer on, of all things, medical grounds, asserting that the frigid open cockpit irritated his rheumatism. Well, maybe so, but in any event it worked.

And so Galland moved to a wing of 109s, commanded by already-famous Werner Moelders. Galland was assigned as adjutant, a non-flying position, but Moelders let him fly the 109 anyway. And when Germany crashed into Holland and Belgium in May of 1940, Galland was flying 109s against France and Britain.

He ran up a score of seven, always eager to get into the air, as one little tale illustrates. On one mission, coming back victorious over a French Potez, he ran out of fuel and landed at the bottom of a hill, short of the runway. Undaunted, he enlisted the aid of a German flak battery to push his airplane up the hill, then coasted and glided down the other side. There he refueled and took off again, after first sending a can of gas to his wing mate, who had committed the same fuelish blunder. His commander's comments are not recorded.

Next came the Battle of Britain, through the long summer of 1940. Here Galland ran into the Spitfire for the first time, and was openly admiring of these sleek airplanes and the men who flew them. The RAF pilots were good and they were aggressive, and they gave at least as good as they got. Galland's score continued to mount, amid vastly exaggerated claims of enemy planes destroyed—on one afternoon Galland's men claimed eight Spitfires destroyed; in fact there were only two.

Galland missed the time the Germans called "The Hardest Day." His day that day was hard enough, for he was listening to *der Dicke* pontificate at his Karinhall estate, handing down the requirement that German single-engined fighters must fly close escort to Messerschmitt Bf 110 twin-engined aircraft. The 110s could not match the Spitfires, to be sure, but requiring the 109s to fly with the 110s gave away any speed advantage, and also meant that combat would have to take place at the altitude most comfortable for the highly maneuverable Spitfire. Galland and Moelders both objected, but got nowhere.

For once Goering was through carping and criticizing his pilots for their failure to protect the bombers, which the RAF was shooting down in numbers. What do you need to win the battle over England, he asked them. Galland gave him a straight answer: "I'd like Spitfires for my squadron." Understandably Goering was far from pleased, but Galland's answer had been neither idle nor disrespectful, but the simple truth: The eight-gun Spitfire was a better fighter at the altitude at which the bombers flew.

As the tide slowly began to turn in the air, Galland led his pilots in opposing the RAF's offensive sweeps over Europe, committing his aircraft in large numbers, attacking the British sweeps from above and when possible out of the sun.

It wasn't all easy. On the 21st of June, he shot down two light bombers, but the Spitfire escort shot him down in turn. He walked away from a crash-landing, then took to the air again in the afternoon; this time he got a Spitfire, but another one shot him up and forced him to bail out. His career almost ended right there; just in time he realized the cord he was pulling was not the ripcord but the parachute harness release. Once he pulled the right cord, he landed wounded but alive.

And then on July 2, he took a cannon round in the armor plate behind his seat. The armor had only been there a few days, and Galland had grumpily chewed out the installer, his mechanic, when Galland hit his head on the new protection. This time the mechanic got profuse thanks.

He even found time for unofficial combat missions, during which he shot down at least one US heavy bomber, perhaps as many as three. Shot down a total of four times himself, he had to suffer the loss of two of his brothers, both aces, both shot down and killed, one by a Royal Air Force Spitfire, the other by an American Thunderbolt.

Galland flew his last mission in mid-November 1941. That month he was pulled off flying combat missions to become general of fighter pilots. He followed Moelders, killed in an air crash. Galland was not happy, but he concentrated on building up the day-fighter arm; he was well aware of the ability of British and Commonwealth pilots, and now the United States was in the war against Germany.

Galland had incurred the wrath of Goering long since—you didn't disagree too loudly or too often with *der Dicke*—but Galland stayed on in his job and did it well with support from people like Albert Speer and even Hitler. Conflict with Goering continued, for Goering tried to insist that every Allied raid be met with a maximum effort, a tactic that Galland knew would quickly wear down the Luftwaffe's greatest asset, its veteran pilots, who had already taken very heavy losses. After all, by now Germany was being hit by American bombers by day and RAF bombers by night.

Over time the argument grew more and more bitter. Galland warned that America would soon be flying fighter escort for her bombers deep into Germany. The two men's falling-out became even more fundamental over Goering's preoccupation with a massive bomber fleet, while Galland clearly understood the urgent need to preserve and expand the fighter force. The two views were incompatible, and by the autumn of 1943, Galland asked to be relieved of his post; Goering first accepted, then changed his mind.

One promising boost for the Luftwaffe's fighter strength came from jet propulsion, especially the Messerschmitt 262, which Galland flew and enthusiastically supported. In the period January to April of 1944, as Galland said, German day-fighters had lost one thousand pilots. That sort of wastage could not continue. But Goering and Hitler were fixated on using the 262 as a bomber. Not until late August did Hitler agree to the formation of an all-jet fighter unit, and even that was badly limited by allocating only one in every twenty built to the fighter arm. It was a drop in the bucket.

Relations with Goering got worse and worse, and now the outspoken Galland and his loyal associates were also the target of the SS and *Gestapo*. The demands of a loyal group of highly decorated pilots on Galland's behalf only made things worse. In the increasingly paranoid, twilight world of dying Nazi Germany, Himmler, who didn't know an airplane from a tricycle, wanted to try Galland for treason.

Finally, Galland was relieved of command in September 1944, for reasons of health of course, the timeworn official excuse. Galland sensibly went to ground in the Harz Mountains but was still in danger, until Hitler heard of it and peremptorily ordered an end to "all this nonsense."

And so it was. Goering listened to his master's voice, and invited Galland to take command of a 262 unit, sixteen jets and fifteen pilots. Galland added seven more aircraft to his total, finishing with a claimed 104 victories.

As the war wound down, Galland clearly saw the coming confrontation between the Russians and the western Allies; he was even willing to add his 262 unit to western airpower to hold back the Reds, but ultimately the tide turned against Germany and he ordered them destroyed.

The long, long war was over.

In a complete change of pace, Galland lived for a time on the estate of Baroness von Donner in Schleswig-Holstein and worked as a forestry worker. He also hunted for the baroness and her children, trading meat for other food at the local market.

But flying was still in his blood, and he next went to Argentina—with the baroness—as a test pilot for designer Kurt Tank's line of new fighters. He even took up gliding again and stayed on in Argentina until 1955; fluent in Spanish, he trained and lectured pilots of the Argentine air force.

Afterward, he returned to Germany, settling in Bonn in 1957 and working as an aircraft consultant. He also worked as a technical advisor in television, performing the same function for the superb film *Battle of Britain*, and appeared at aviation events such as the US Air Force's Gathering of Eagles program. Along the way he found time to write his autobiographical *The First and the Last*, which sold several million copies.

He became and remained friends with cherished old enemies like RAF aces Douglas Bader and Robert Stanford Tuck. And in 1983 he sought and found his mechanic, he of the armor-plated headrest, and that year and every year thereafter, the mechanic and his wife were invited to the Galland home.

Galland's health gradually declined, until his death in early February 1996. He had achieved much, some of it fighting for a rotten cause, but throughout he had kept his soul and his honor intact.

CHAPTER THIRTY

Faith, Hope, and Charity: The Battle for Malta

THE ANCIENT CHRISTIAN CHURCH HAD THREE SAINTS CALLED FAITH, Hope, and Charity, and of course those qualities were considered the cardinal virtues of any Christian person. But in the peculiar way of men at war, those holy words later became names for three venerable British biplane fighters, gallant crates charged with the defense of a tiny, critical island in the Mediterranean against huge odds.

The Gladiator's top speed was only about 250 miles per hour, but it was highly maneuverable and had a closed cockpit and four guns in .303 caliber. It was a sturdy machine for all its antique design, and did much damage to its countries' enemies in experienced hands; South African RAF ace Marmaduke "Pat" Pattle, for example, flew a Gladiator to fifteen victories.

Some legends of the epic defense of Malta have Faith, Hope, and Charity fighting all alone against Axis raids on the island. There were more than three Gladiators based in Malta, although it may be that the tiny air force was indeed briefly reduced below three one or more times. Other fighters also rose to defend Malta, Hurricanes and Spitfires among them, but these famous three obsolescent biplanes were a symbol for all the gallantry of the RAF during the siege; they still are.

Perhaps the names were coined and stuck because of the hard times they described. The years 1941 and 1942 were difficult ones for the Allies, who everywhere were on the defensive, up against the monstrous airpower of both Italy's Regia Aeronautica and the German Luftwaffe. The island of Malta was a critical part of the defense, for from it the Allies struck Axis shipping in the Mediterranean, shipping that was critical to the *Afrika Korps'* drive along the north African littoral toward Egypt and the critically important Suez Canal.

Germany and Italy responded. Plans were laid for a joint invasion of Malta—a foray named by the Germans somewhat grandiosely *Herkules*—including an assault from the sky by German *Fallschirmjäger* (paratroopers). A protracted attack by aircraft would soften up the defenses first: The two Axis air forces mounted a phenomenal three thousand raids over two years in preparation for the invasion that would never come.

British aircraft and the Royal Navy stood in the way, and would stay there. But both the navy and the merchant marine took hideous casualties keeping the Union Jack flying above Malta; so did the very gallant civilian population, which "carried on" much as the people back in England had survived the Blitz.

So protracted and heavy were Axis air strikes that for a time— roughly June to December 1941—the British used some of their larger submarines as transport, running vital supplies into Malta. During that period RN subs made sixteen such trips, carrying medical supplies, aviation fuel, kerosene, mail, and a few vital personnel. These runs continued until November of the next year.

There had been no Malta convoys from the west since the fall of Crete in the spring of 1941, in the face of the enormous Luftwaffe strength that cost the Royal Navy and the merchant ships very heavy casualties. By July of 1942 thirteen ships had been run in from Alexandria, but heavier supply and reinforcement was needed. And so in July a six-ship convoy was scheduled, escorted as heavily as the Navy could manage. Losses had reduced the available ships to carrier *Ark Royal*, battle cruiser *Renown*, cruiser *Hermione*, minelayer *Manxman*, battleship *Nelson*, three cruisers, and eleven destroyers.

The big ships would travel east as far as the Sicilian Narrows, then wait for the smaller ships' return while they escorted the convoy through the last desperate dash to Malta. It was a daunting prospect, for the main Italian fleet had four battleships and three cruiser divisions available.

Ultimately however, the Italians attacked only from the air and with a small force of torpedo boats. The big ships stayed in port.

The British had driven the convoy through with the loss of only a single destroyer and moderate damage to two other ships. Fairey Fulmar fighter aircraft from *Ark Royal* shot down several of the attackers and damaged others. Admiral Somerville summed up the successful run concisely: "It was an amazing affair. They had Palermo and Messina packed with cruisers and destroyers and not a move! And so home to bed."

Another Malta resupply run in late September—this one called *Halberd*—came through when the Italian fleet, sailing to intercept, discovered that the British fleet contained not one battleship, but three; the Italians wanted no part of those odds, called off the battle, and returned to port. Meanwhile, Axis convoys were suffering badly from air strikes by RAF Blenheim light bombers by day and Swordfish torpedo attacks by night.

The pendulum was now swinging the other way. Rommel was feeling the shortage of supplies in October of 1941, preparing another North African offensive. The Italian navy, under army urging, prepared a seven-freighter convoy, covered by six destroyers as close escort and a covering force of two heavy cruisers and four more destroyers. To warn of any British reaction, several submarines haunted the sea around Malta.

The Italian navy saw nothing that night; they missed the departure of cruisers *Aurora* and *Penelope* and destroyers *Lance* and *Lively* from Valetta. Until, that is, the shells began to fall around them. One destroyer lasted only a few minutes and a second was dead in the water. All the supply vessels were sent to the bottom, and while what remained of the escort was running for home, HMS *Upholder* torpedoed and sank still another destroyer.

It got worse. In September of 1941, 28 percent of cargoes to Libya were sunk; it was 21 percent in November and rose to a catastrophic 63 percent in December.

But Hitler was fulminating at his officers to regain "air and sea mastery between southern Italy and Cyrenaica. The suppression of Malta is particularly important." And so the long fight was on again.

German submarines and aircraft were part of the catastrophe, but worse was an uncharted Axis minefield that cost the Royal Navy a cruiser and a destroyer sunk and two cruisers damaged. And the Italian navy did what it did best, sinking *Valiant* and *Queen Elizabeth* in harbor with two-frogman "pigs" or "chariots." The British were the first to acknowledge the daring and cold courage of the Italian crews, both of whom became prisoners of war.

But now Japan was in the war, and more losses came to the Royal Navy and the US Navy, losses that could not be made up quickly and meant that the lost resources could not be moved to European waters.

Things were bad enough on Malta, the bull's-eye of Goering's Luftwaffe. For three months, starting in December 1941 and continuing into March and April of 1942, the Axis aircraft went on hammering at the island. But in March the British carrier force flew in fifteen Spitfires, followed by fifteen more. And on March 20 another supply convoy sailed for Malta, helped by diversionary actions including deep raids on German airfields by the Long Range Desert Group.

But this time the Italian surface ships persisted, and Admiral Vian threw his little escort in harm's way, 5.25- and 4.7-inch guns against the Italians' fifteen-, eight-, and six-inch guns. The heroics of Vian's little force brought the convoy home, but most of its cargo was lost to heavy German bombing not long after it reached Malta.

Malta's ordeal went on through April, when between the 15th and 30th, the island fought off 115 raids. Reinforcements of Spitfires were largely destroyed on the ground, at least until May 9, when carriers *Wasp* and *Eagle* flew in sixty Spitfires. They arrived in the middle of a *Fliegerkorps* raid, but the ground crews got them into the air, refueled and armed, some as quickly as thirty-five minutes after arriving. From this time the German raiders took steadily increasing losses.

For long periods any of Malta's submarines in port had spent much of their time submerged in their own harbor, at the height of the frequent Italian and German raids. They could not be moved to another, safer anchorage farther away; their role in making hostile shipping lanes untenable was too important, under perhaps the most difficult, dangerous submarine waters on earth, the Mediterranean, known as "the Med." An example was the short, spectacular careers of Capt. David Wanklyn and his command, HMS *Upholder.*

The brief histories of this submarine and skipper ran fifteen hair-raising months, during which they sank a destroyer, a minesweeper, and a record *three* enemy submarines, plus badly damaging a light cruiser, sinking eleven merchantmen, and damaging four more. It was a remarkable feat in relatively shallow waters, full of Axis mines and under virtually constant observation by enemy aircraft, for those busy waters were the Axis powers' only highway to vital North Africa. Return to port brought little release or even sleep, for the Axis aircraft staged multiple raids nearly every day.

The brilliant careers of Wanklyn and *Upholder* extended to twenty-eight patrols, but on that last patrol, *Upholder* simply disappeared, gone without a trace. It is probable that the disappearance was the work of German aircraft and Italian surface vessels, but nobody knows for certain. It might well have been a mine, for the Mediterranean was sown thick with them, and there was no message from the gallant Wanklyn to give even a clue to their passing. There never would be again.

At last, by mid-July of 1942, Rommel had shot his bolt, and the British Eighth Army would be reinforced by a shipment of three hundred Sherman tanks and some one hundred 105-millimeter self-propelled guns. German and Italian air raids were costing the attackers about twice as many aircraft as the defenders lost. The tide was turning.

The tide crested in late May 1942, with the beginning of the fight at El Alamein, where an initial German-Italian multi-division attack was defeated and the British Eighth Army began the offensive that would drive the Germans out of North Africa.

Significantly also, the end of May marked the start of a new era for RAF bombing of Germany. Two German targets, the Ruhr and Koeln, were hammered by raids of well over a thousand aircraft. It was a preview of what was on the way. Germany was finding out the bitter truth about sowing the wind.

And the famous trinity of Gladiators?

Charity was shot down on the last day of July 1940. Her pilot, though badly burned, survived. *Hope* was destroyed on the ground in May 1941. *Faith*, the last of the three, survived to rest quietly in Malta's

War Museum. At least the fuselage is there, including parts from "at least one other Gladiator," and a continuing struggle goes on to marry up the fuselage with a set of Gladiator wings in Malta's Aviation Museum.

However that competition is resolved, the gallant memory lives on.

CHAPTER THIRTY-ONE

The Boys from Shangri-La

In Which Jimmie Doolittle Visits Tokyo Uninvited

THE SPRING OF 1942 WAS NOT A HAPPY TIME FOR THE UNITED STATES and her allies. America had lost the Philippines; Britain had lost Malaya and was falling back in Burma; Holland had lost her possessions in the Dutch East Indies. Naval losses for all three nations had been heavy, and many people were deeply concerned with the vital short-term need to salvage whatever could be saved from the ruin. And all of these nations had Hitler's rampant Germany to contend with, plus her arrogant ally, Italy, in addition to Japan.

But some of those same people already had their thoughts and dreams focused on something else, something far more satisfying: revenge. Admiral Yamamoto, the able architect of Japan's aggression in the Pacific, had put it perfectly in responding to congratulations on Japan's successful attack on the Hawaiian Islands. "I fear," he said, "that all we have done is awaken a sleeping giant." He was, as most Americans would say, right on the money.

President Roosevelt was one of those intent on striking back, and the sooner the better. And so, just two weeks after the sneak attack on Pearl Harbor, in a meeting with the Joint Chiefs of Staff at the White House, he voiced his notion that the United States should bomb Japan as soon as possible, in order to boost American morale. Planning began immediately.

Since there was no base close enough to Japan from which to fly off bombers against the home islands of Imperial Japan, it became obvious that the raiders would have to come by sea. Taking off from one of the Navy's carriers might just be possible, with some modifications of the bombers and a lot of luck. The raiders would have to be multi-engined bombers, and those belonged to the Army Air Corps. The Navy's aircraft carriers would have to sail deep into the Pacific, dangerously close to Japan's home waters, if the Army's bombers were to carry a decent bomb load and have any chance of flying from their targets on to some place of reasonable safety where the crews might survive.

For the bombers could not return to the carrier from which they had been launched, even if they could manage a carrier landing, a problematical possibility itself. The carriers would have to clear out at high speed once they had launched the strike. Waters that close to Japan were far too dangerous, and America's small carrier force was far too precious to risk by loitering for most of a day so near Japan. In order to reach Japan from any distance with a decent load of bombs—a half ton per plane was the goal—the multi-engined Army aircraft had to be capable of taking off from a carrier flight deck.

No four-engined bomber would even fit on a carrier flight deck, let alone take off from one. So it would have to be a medium bomber, and the planners carefully looked over the available aircraft. Two types were rejected because their wingspan was too broad for the carrier; in the end the planners settled on the B-25 Mitchell. It was twice tested, and both times took off successfully from USS *Hornet*.

Work began immediately on major modifications. The interior changes to the plane were mostly to accommodate extra gas tanks to almost double the bomber's regular fuel capacity, but there were more. The treasured Norden bombsight was replaced by a crude device dreamed up by one of the pilots, called the "Mark Twain" and costing a whole twenty cents. The belly turret and one radio were removed to save weight, and a pair of dummy guns were added to the stern of each B-25.

Starting on the first of March, the crews began rehearsals in Florida, flying at night and over water, practicing low-altitude bombing and takeoffs from a section of runway painted in the shape and size of a carrier deck. And on the 1st of April, 1942, sixteen modified bombers were loaded on *Hornet* at Alameda Naval Air Station on San Francisco Bay. Each aircraft had a crew of five, and a two-hundred-man maintenance and support detachment went to sea with them.

Next day the task force sailed, out into the broad Pacific: *Hornet*, sister-ship *Enterprise*—providing fighter cover for the little task force—and three heavy and one light cruisers, eight destroyers, and two fleet oilers. On the 17th the oilers refueled everybody, and then they and the destroyers turned for home. The carriers and cruisers pushed on at high speed for their launching point in the dangerous seas east of Japan.

They were unobserved most of the way, but on the morning of April 18, the little fleet ran into a Japanese picketboat, *Nitto Maru*. Light cruiser *Nashville* promptly sent *Nitto Maru* to the bottom, but she had gotten off a radio signal before she sank. On the correct assumption that the presence of American ships was now known by the Japanese naval command, Capt. (later Admiral) Mark Mitscher of *Hornet* made a hard but wise decision. He would launch the strike immediately, although the task force was still some 170 nautical miles short of the planned launch point, and ten hours ahead of schedule.

All sixteen B-25's got into the air in everybody's first real carrier takeoff. Each bomber carried three 250-pound bombs and a bundle of incendiaries, rigged to break apart and scatter over a broad area once it was dropped. Several bombs had medals attached to them, Japanese "friendship medals" given to Americans in a less hostile time. Now they would be returned . . . with interest.

Flying in at "zero feet," Doolittle's men arrived over Japan and split up, their coming apparently a complete surprise to the Japanese defenders in spite of the little picketboat's radio warning. There was some light anti-aircraft fire and attacks by a few fighters, as the bombers struck at ten targets in Tokyo, two more in Yokohoma, and one each in Nagoya, Kobe, Yokosuka, and Osaka. Only one B-25 was damaged, and gunners on *Hara Karier* got two Japanese fighters; *Whirling Dervish* shot down another one. The bombers' nose gunners sprayed everything in sight, and the force was gone into the west, as suddenly as it had come.

The raid's planners had laid out a course southwest across the East China Sea that would bring the aircraft over China in about twelve hours. There were bases there that could receive them, primarily at a place called Zhuzhou, for which fifteen of the bombers headed. The sixteenth aircraft was gobbling gasoline at a frightening rate, and its commander wisely elected to turn for the closer Soviet Union, landing near Vladivostok. The Russians had a problem: At the time they had a non-aggression pact with Japan, so they decided they could not honor a request from the United States to release the crew. The American crew was therefore interned; well-treated, but still not free. That is, until they were moved to a town near the Iranian border.

There the plane commander managed to bribe a man he thought was a smuggler, who got the Americans across the border into sanctuary at a British consulate. It much later developed that the providential "smuggling" was in fact the work of the Soviets' NKVD law enforcement agency, achieving clandestinely what their government could not legally do in the cold light of day.

The other crews either bailed out or crash-landed in China. They got much unselfish help from the Chinese, soldiers and civilians alike, and also from an American missionary. Sixty-nine men escaped the Japanese; three were killed in action when their B-25 crashed and a fourth died when he fell from a cliff after bailing out. Two crews were missing and unaccounted for, until, in August, the Swiss consul in Shanghai advised that two crew members had drowned after their aircraft landed at sea, and the other eight were prisoners of the Japanese.

In August the Japanese announced that all eight had been "tried" and sentenced to death, although several sentences had been commuted, they said, to life in prison. In fact, three Americans were shot by firing squad. The rest were imprisoned on starvation rations. One man died; the remaining emaciated aircrew were freed by American troops in August 1945. Remarkably, one of those four, Corp. Jacob DeShazer, later returned to Japan as a missionary, and served there for more than thirty years. Greater love hath no man.

The raid was a tremendous psychological blow to Japan, although as predicted, the material damage was relatively light. Until now the holy home islands were thought to be safe from the inferior westerners. By contrast, the delight in America overflowed, a bright ray of sunshine for a country deeply angry at the nation that smiled and talked peace even while its carriers were steaming into position to strike at Pearl Harbor. One of the authors still remembers his father's comment when the news of the raid on Japan broke: "Take that, you bastards!"

Not only in Japan, but all across America, people asked, "where did the American bombers come from?"

Why, from Shangri-La, said President Roosevelt, using the name of the hidden mountain paradise created in James Hilton's classic novel *Lost Horizon*. The Japanese navy tried hard to find the American ships from which they knew the raid was launched, but they only managed to add to their embarrassment. Even though they used five carriers and a multitude of other ships, they still failed to find the American task force, let alone attack it, adding to the great shame of allowing the enemy to penetrate so deeply into the holy waters of Imperial Japan in the first place.

The dark side of the raid was the predictable Japanese reaction in China, especially in the eastern coastal provinces that could harbor American airmen as they did the Doolittle raiders. Operation *Seigo* did its evil best to ensure that no Chinese who helped the American raiders would ever do so again. The generally accepted civilian death toll from Japanese reprisals was ten thousand. Other estimates run as high as a quarter of a million.

There was an unexpected consequence, too. There is a suggestion that the strike on Japan may have reinforced Adm. Isoroku Yamamoto's decision to strike at Midway Island, or at least forced his hand on timing, setting the stage for the US Navy's decisive whipping of the Japanese in June of 1942. Midway was a startling, massive American victory, gutting Japan's carrier force and, maybe more importantly, destroying much of her cadre of experienced carrier pilots.

America rejoiced at the daring raid on the Japanese homeland. Jimmie Doolittle, who thought he might be court-martialed for losing his entire command, instead received the Congressional Medal of Honor and was promoted two grades to brigadier general.

The bombs didn't do much damage; nobody expected them to. But while Japan was deeply ashamed and could never feel secure again, America smiled. And one small step had been taken toward the far-off day of complete retribution. Japan had sowed the wind at Pearl Harbor. Four years later a big, sleek bomber named *Enola Gay* would bring the very fires of hell to the islands of Japan.

Chapter Thirty-Two

The Great Marianas Turkey Shoot

After more than thirty months of war, the Japanese government still adhered to its original war plan: If America's military forces could be subjected to sufficiently high casualty rates, the American public would finally force its government to sue for peace. That attitude had not changed in the spring of 1944, even after Japan's disastrous loss at Midway, the methodical march of America up the Solomon Islands chain, and the successful British stand in Burma.

The real genius of Japan's operations at sea, Adm. Isoroku Yamamoto, was dead, his aircraft shot down by an American P-38 fighter over Bougainville on April 18, 1943. Even worse, Japanese losses in aircraft and experienced pilots had been very heavy, as the American offensive moved inexorably across the Pacific. Also dead was his successor, Admiral Koga, and the saving of Japan fell to Adm. Soemu Toyoda.

By early June of 1944, he had put the finishing touches on Operation *A-Go*. The massive American naval strength was headed for the Mariana Island chain, which included Saipan, Tinian, and Guam. The Japanese were outnumbered in carriers, fifteen to nine, but could count on land-based aircraft to supplement the carriers, and on the Japanese capability of landing their carrier aircraft on strips ashore and then shuttling back and forth to the carriers. At least some of their aircraft had a range greater than their American opponents, which meant the Japanese could engage American ships before US aircraft could reach the Imperial fleet.

In June 1944 American air strikes began in the Marianas; the Japanese had expected the American strike to come elsewhere, and had only fifty land-based combat aircraft stationed there. By the 15th, American landings began on Saipan, capture of which would put US B-29 bombers within range of the Japanese home islands. The Japanese responded by attacking.

Adm. Raymond Spruance, commanding the American fleet, had to make an agonizing decision. He could nullify the Japanese advantage in range by closing the range during the night, but he quite rightly adhered to his orders that his primary task was to cover the invasion fleet. And early in the morning of the 19th, a Japanese plane from Guam found and reported the position of the American force; the pilot then attacked a destroyer and was shot down, but now the battle had been fully joined.

The Japanese flew off aircraft from Guam and other islands, but they were met by some thirty Grumman F6F Hellcats. The American fighters shot down thirty-five Japanese aircraft for the loss of just one of their own. Then, about 10:00 a.m., the Japanese came again in strength. Admiral Mitscher scrambled all available fighters, and even flew off his bombers to clear the carriers in case some of the Japanese got through.

The first wave of Japanese paused to regroup their squadrons at about seventy miles out, and Mitscher's aircraft met them there. Another wild dogfight followed, which the Americans won again, hands-down, twenty-five planes to one. The Japanese survivors ran into more American fighters and lost another sixteen planes. A handful broke through, and one of them got a bomb onto USS *South Dakota*, killing or injuring some sixty men, but no Japanese aircraft got as far as the American carriers. *South Dakota* went right on with her duties, serving as a huge floating anti-aircraft battery.

About 11:00 a.m., still another mass attack came in, over a hundred planes, which achieved nothing but a few casualties on two American carriers. This one cost the Japanese ninety-seven more aircraft, and still another at about 1:00 p.m. cost the Japanese another seven. A fourth Japanese strike launched at around 11:00 a.m., given an incorrect position, failed to even find the American fleet, until one segment stumbled on American ships and lost a further nine aircraft.

Meanwhile, fighting continued over Orote airstrip on Guam, where American pilots had jumped forty-nine enemy aircraft trying to land. They shot down thirty of them and left the rest, as one source put it, "damaged beyond repair." It was in reference to this last stunning victory that a pilot on carrier *Lexington* said, "Hell, this is like an old-time turkey shoot!"

Japanese losses on this single day exceeded 350, as against about thirty American aircraft, and now the Silent Service (United States Pacific Fleet) was about to do its spectacular best. USS *Albacore* launched a six-fish salvo at carrier *Taiho*. Four torpedoes missed, and a Japanese pilot saw the wake of one of the remaining torpedoes and crashed his aircraft into it. So *Albacore* got only one hit from her broadside, but that was enough.

Taiho gradually filled with gas fumes from ruptured fuel tanks, making a huge bomb, and finally sparks from a generator ignited the fumes. Of the 2,150 men aboard, 1,650 went down with the ship.

USS *Cavalla* torpedoed carrier *Shokaku*, again rupturing tanks of aviation gas. *Shokaku* literally blew up, taking to the bottom with her more than twelve hundred men. Both American submarines suffered some depth-charge damage, but both eluded the Japanese.

Mitscher pushed west during the night, and flew out patrols at dawn to find his quarry. Vice-Admiral Ozawa was still aggressive, especially considering his enormous losses in aircraft, but he decided to carry on attacking with the new day. He had only about 150 serviceable aircraft left, but he thought there were still more to draw from on Rota and Guam.

Mitscher's searches paid off in mid-afternoon, when a plane from the carrier *Enterprise* found the Japanese ships. The enemy was running west, almost out of range, but the admiral decided to strike and launched. Then came the word that his target was sixty miles farther away than first reported.

Mitscher recalled all his attacking aircraft except the first wave; they still had a chance to strike the enemy, although it would be at extreme range, and on their return they would have to land in the dark. And so 226 aircraft bored in to find the Japanese: ninety-five Hellcats, the rest a mixture of dive-bombers and torpedo planes. Well aware of their fuel shortage, the pilots attacked as quickly as possible. Carrier *Hiyo* went down with 250 men, and the attackers damaged three more carriers, big battleship *Haruna*, and a couple of tankers. The cost was twenty American warplanes, fallen to anti-aircraft and Japanese fighters.

The flight back was harrowing, for night fell before the strike force could reach friendly ships. In the darkness, just before 9:00 p.m., the first of them began coming home. Mitscher had broken custom by authorizing anybody to land anywhere they could, home carrier or not. And then the admiral took a long and courageous chance and directed his carriers to light up the night, shining search lights into the heavens to mark the way home. Destroyers fired star shells to help guide the lost sheep to the barn.

Mitscher ignored the chance of a Japanese submarine or aircraft homing in on all this light to attack; he would not abandon his aircrew in that uncertain night. As a result, most of the returning force managed to land on somebody's flight deck or ditch close enough to be picked up that night or later by ships and aircraft combing the area for them. Eighty aircraft didn't make it back; most of the crews did.

Those two days off the Marianas were the last hurrah of Japanese naval aviation. Most of what was left of their experienced pilots were gone now, along with five to six hundred aircraft. There remained the Battle of Leyte Gulf, another big win for the United States . . . but the Japanese navy—especially its air arm—had been gutted in the Marianas.

CHAPTER THIRTY-THREE

The Nelson Touch

Swordfish at Taranto

The Swordfish fly over the ocean
The Swordfish fly over the sea;
If were not for King George's Swordfish
where the 'ell would the Fleet Air Arm be?

—PILOTS' SONG

IN THE LATE AUTUMN OF 1940, GREAT BRITAIN, HER EMPIRE AND THE Commonwealth, stood at bay, opposing all alone the massive power of Germany and Italy. The Royal Air Force had won the Battle of Britain, throwing back the much larger Luftwaffe in the skies above England. At the same time the British army was rebuilding after the miracle of Dunkirk, and British troops were driving the Italians out of Eritrea.

In spite of these successes against the Axis, however, long-term British prospects were grim, especially across the oceans of the world. The British Admiralty fully understood that in the end the war would be won or lost at sea. The convoy routes to the Americas had to be kept open at any cost, whatever else happened. At the same time the Royal Navy had to keep control of the Mediterranean, for if Britain could not hold the Med, then everything east of Gibraltar became an Italian lake, and the Axis would be able to pour supplies into North Africa.

And if the North African littoral were to be lost, almost surely Egypt and the Suez Canal would follow. If that happened, Britain would be cut off from India and from the vital oil of the Middle East, save by the terribly long and dangerous route around the Cape, up through the south Atlantic and around the shoulder of occupied France to the islands of Britain.

The key to interdicting Axis supplies to North Africa was the stubborn little island of Malta, for the successful defense of which the Royal Navy and the Maltese civilian population would make enormous sacrifices over the next two years. Without Royal Navy support Malta would fall, its submarines and aircraft would have to be withdrawn, and German and Italian convoys could reinforce Axis units in North Africa at will. And if the Italian air force at present lacked a really first-class bombing capability, British intelligence was well aware that failing would be remedied by the aircraft of the Luftwaffe.

And as if hordes of enemy aircraft and German and Italian submarines were not enough to contend with, the British were faced with the threat of a large Italian surface fleet. For strutting dictator Benito Mussolini, eager to create a modern-day replica of the Roman Empire, had poured great sums of money into building a modern fleet. The Mediterranean will be *mare nostrum*, he boasted, "our sea," and he had gone a long way toward realizing his dream.

By autumn of 1940 the Italians had six battleships ready for action or almost so. *Littorio* and *Vittorio Veneto*, about ready for sea, were brand-new big-gun ships, faster than the World War I–vintage British battleships and able to outrange all of them except for *Warspite* and *Valiant*. Already at sea the Italians had two newly modernized 12.6-inch-gun battleships—*Cavour* and *Giulio Cesare*—both of which were fitted with anti-submarine bulges below the waterline. Two more battleships of the *Doria* class—*Andrea Doria* and *Caio Duillio*—were finishing up their sea trials.

In addition, the Italians fielded at least nineteen cruisers, seven of which were heavy, sixty-one fleet destroyers, sixty-nine other destroyers and big torpedo boats, and 105 submarines, then the largest undersea fleet in the world. The Royal Navy was outnumbered in the Med, but early encounters favored the British. In a July fleet action, HMS *Warspite* hit battleship *Giulio Cesare* with a fifteen-inch shell, and the Italians broke off the action and ran for home. Ten days later cruiser HMAS *Sydney* and her destroyers took on two Italian cruisers and sank one of them, *Bartolomo Colleoni*. And then, in September, light cruiser HMS *Ajax*—one of the victors over pocket-battleship *Graf Spee* in 1939—was attacked by a small flotilla of Italian destroyers. The cruiser's superb gunnery routed the attackers, sinking three and damaging still another. *Ajax* suffered only minor damage.

Stretched thin all across the world, charged with covering vital Malta, with protecting British convoys in the Med, and with interdicting Italian convoys to North Africa, the Royal Navy had its hands full. Sir Andrew Cunningham, the Scottish admiral commanding in the Mediterranean, determined to even the odds, and he would rely on one weapon the Italians could not match: his two aircraft carriers, *Illustrious* and *Eagle*.

Cunningham was the quintessential British sea-dog, heir to the great tradition of Drake and Raleigh, Nelson and Beatty. His penetrating blue eyes missed nothing, and he was famous for his encyclopedic memory for the faces of men who had served with him in the past. Even in the darkest days of the war, Cunningham never lost his confidence or his spirit, and he would not tolerate any man who did not share his driving aggressiveness and perpetual optimism.

Throughout World War II, the operations of the Royal Navy would be characterized by daring and aggressiveness. The weathered gray ships of Britain gave battle at every opportunity, fought against long odds again and again—and generally won. Now, with Mediterranean naval hegemony in the balance, Admiral Cunningham was precisely the man to carry the fight to the Axis.

Cunningham was the right man for the time and the place. His ships would continue to beat the Italians again and again, notably in a night fleet action off Cape Matapan in March of 1941. On that night his ships would sink Italian cruisers *Zara*, *Fliume*, and *Pola*, plus a pair of destroyers, and badly damage big *Vittorio Veneto*, all without British losses. That was in the future, however, and now, facing an increasing Italian surface threat, Cunningham would not, could not, wait for the Italian menace to put to sea. He would carry the fight to the enemy's backyard. Cunningham's Mediterranean fleet would attack nothing less than the heart of the Italian fleet—its anchorage at Taranto, just inside the heel of the boot of Italy.

The hammer of Cunningham's fleet was the modern carrier *Illustrious*, sister to *Victorious* and *Formidable*, and her complement of torpedo aircraft, the astonishing Fairey Swordfish. The Swordfish was the end product of several unsatisfactory interwar designs, complicated by a dispute within the Admiralty about the relative merits of bombing and torpedo attack. The torpedo enthusiasts won that round, perhaps relying on a sound maxim attributed to an American admiral: "It's much more effective to let water in through the bottom than air through the top."

The Swordfish ranks with the most remarkable fighting machines in the history of warfare. Affectionately called the "stringbag" by her aircrews, the Swordfish looked like a leftover from World War I. She was a fabric-covered biplane, for one thing, an anachronism in this day of sleek, single-wing aircraft. Her two wings were braced with a forest of wires, and her three-man crew flew in open cockpits.

At the start of the war, the Royal Navy had thirteen Swordfish squadrons, plus a handful more rigged as float planes, designed to be catapulted from warships. The Swordfish was slow, capable of no more than a lumbering 138 miles per hour, and she was distinctly under-armed, carrying only a single rifle-caliber machine gun firing forward and a Lewis gun in her rear cockpit. By comparison with the torpedo aircraft of other nations, she was an obsolete machine that should have been little more than a superb target for anti-aircraft . . . but she was all the Royal Navy had, and she would prove to be a remarkable performer.

Her crews liked her—she was solid and reliable, and she handled easily. Her relatively short range—about 450 miles at the outset—would improve with the mounting of auxiliary fuel tanks, shipped out to the Mediterrean in *Illustrious*. The Swordfish carried a twelve-hundred-pound torpedo, substantially the same weapon fielded in World War I. By the fall of 1940, however, a new and deadly feature was added to the old weapon.

For the first time the British fish were armed with the Duplex pistol, which provided an extra dimension. In the usual way, the Duplex detonator would fire the torpedo on contact with an Italian ship, but it would also explode the fish if it passed beneath the magnetic field of an enemy vessel's hull. British torpedo experts on *Illustrious*, planning for the attack in the constricted, shallow harbor of Taranto, also did a little extra tinkering with their weapons:

> *It was decided to run off 100 yards of the safety range [so that the torpedo would arm more quickly] and the battery resistance was removed to ensure that the torpedoes would remain dangerous on completion of their run.*

Which left a safety margin of just three hundred yards. The British set their torpedoes to run at thirty-three feet, which would prove to be about seven feet deeper than the bottom strand of the Italian torpedo nets. The Italians had not counted on the Duplex torpedo pistols.

During the prewar crisis in Ethiopia, Royal Navy staff officers had worked out a plan for attacking the Italian base at Taranto. And now Rear Admiral Lumbey St. G. Lyster, commanding carrier *Glorious* in this autumn of 1940, dusted off the old plans. Now called Operation Judgment, they were incorporated in a larger and more complex matrix called Operation M.B. 8. The Taranto operation had to go in within a window of several nights during which moonlight would be available to light the attackers' way.

M.B. 8 was a mammoth and complex operation, of which the Taranto strike was only a part. A number of separate naval forces would participate. To start with, the British would send four convoys to sea at once, each covered by warships. Five merchantmen would make the run from Alexandria, Egypt, to Malta, accompanied partway by two more ships that would leave the convoy to run troops and supplies into Suda Bay on Crete. Three more ships would carry precious fuel from Egypt to Greece. Four large vessels, sailing empty, would sail from Malta for Alexandria, and four more empties bound from Greece and Turkey would head for Alexandria.

Meanwhile, Force F, heavy fleet reinforcements, including battleship *Barham*, would sail east from Gibraltar (this part of the plan was called Operation Coat), carrying troop reinforcements on board. They would be covered on the way by Vice-Admiral Sir James Somerville's Force H, which included carrier *Ark Royal*.

Once all of the convoys were safely home, Cunningham's main strength—Force A—would turn toward Taranto, and a separate force would set off toward the Straits of Otranto, up the Adriatic between Italy and Greece, to savage whatever Italian merchantmen and warships it might find. The small British force given this task—Force X—was commanded by an admiral with the oddly mellifluous name of Pridham-Wippel. Though his name may have sounded a little foppish, Pridham-Wippel was another sea-dog cut from the the same cloth as Cunningham. He would sail in *Leander*-class light cruiser *Orion*, followed by sister-ships *Ajax* and HMAS *Sydney*, in company with tribal-class destroyers *Nubian* and *Mohawk*.

Cunningham, with all of this going on, would sail his carrier strike-force to a central position in the Med, from which he could cover all of this multitude of forces in case the Italians sortied, and make contact with the fleet reinforcements headed east from Gibraltar. On the 7th and 8th, he would also be joined by light cruisers *Ajax* and *Sydney*, which had successfully run reinforcements and equipment into Crete.

All of the planning and execution for the Taranto strike depended on accurate and timely intelligence, accurate photos showing the state of the port's defenses and, in particular, the number and type of ships anchored there and their positions. A bit of luck would help as well. Up to the autumn of 1940, the British had lacked a long-range aircraft fast enough to fly into the teeth of the enemy's lair, take its photos, and get out.

This lack was remedied by the arrival at Malta of three twin-engined Martin Marylands. Called "Bob Martins" by their fond crews, they were in crates on their way to the French forces when France fell. Redirected into British hands, they now flew regular missions over Taranto and other Italian ports. Admiral Cunningham would know precisely what his men would face. By contrast, the Italian reconnaissance crews were stuck with outmoded Cant Z501 and Z506 seaplanes: The Italian pilots' nickname for the Z501 was "Mama help me!"

On November 6, 1940, *Illustrious* sailed from Alexandria with twenty-four Swordfish on board, including five aircraft and eight crews from *Eagle*, out of action with a faulty fuel-delivery system. *Illustrious* was commanded by Capt. Denis Boyd, a pilot himself. On board was Admiral Lyster, now appointed Rear Admiral, Aircraft Carriers, Mediterranean.

On the 8th of November, Cunningham's strike force met the Malta-bound five-ship convoy, and *Illustrious's* fighter aircraft took up the task of holding off Italian air reconnaissance. One Italian reconnaissance plane was driven away by a couple of obsolete Gladiator biplanes. The same performance was repeated later in the day, and in late afternoon seven Italian bombers appeared. This time they were taken on by three two-seater, eight-gun Fulmar fighters, which shot down two of them. The rest dumped their bombs in the sea and ran for home.

The next day Italian aircraft neared Force A on four occasions. A Fulmar got one and the others fled, but the Italians surely knew now that the heart of the British fleet was at sea, and where it was. And on that day one of carrier *Eagle's* aircraft flying from *Illustrious* crash-landed in the sea—the crew were saved—one of three *Eagle* Swordfish that would be lost to bad gasoline before the flight to Taranto ever began.

At midday on the 10th, Force A sighted the four-ship convoy from Malta to Alexandria, escorted by battleship *Ramillies*, cruiser *Coventry*, and two destroyers. By late afternoon that convoy was safe, and now Cunningham could turn his attention to the last remaining tasks of the whole operation: the raid on shipping in Otranto Straits . . . and the strike on Taranto. Force A pressed eastward, and by noon on the next day, the 11th, was about midway between Malta and Crete.

At 6:00 p.m., the Taranto strike force—*Illustrious* covered by four cruisers, two heavy and two light, and four destroyers—was detached. Admiral Lyster, now commanding from *Illustrious*, steamed for the position chosen to launch the attack, just west of the Greek island of Cephalonia. With the heavy ships Cunningham would cover both operations.

The heart of Cunningham's strike force was *Illustrious*. The original attack plan had called for the use of twenty-two-year-old carrier *Eagle* in addition, but *Eagle* had suffered so much damage from near-miss bombs in earlier actions that her gasoline pumping system was non-functional and could not be repaired in time. Force A also included battleships *Warspite*, *Valiant*, and *Malaya*, covered by cruisers *Gloucester* and *York* and thirteen destroyers.

The Royal Navy was traditionally aggressive and had long been. Lord Nelson had put it pretty well in his fighting instructions before Trafalgar: "No captain can go far wrong if he places his ship alongside one of the enemy." The resources available for a strike at the heart of the Italian mainland were, however, frighteningly meager. This single carrier would have to provide the strike force, just twenty-one aircraft instead of the originally planned thirty, attacking a major port defended by no fewer than twenty-one batteries of four-inch anti-aircraft guns and some two hundred AA machine guns, plus the enormous volume of fire to be expected from the anti-aircraft guns of six battleships, nine cruisers, and a great bevy of destroyers and smaller warships.

RAF Malta's Marylands, with the range and the speed to provide accurate and timely intelligence on the Italian fleet, produced brilliant pictures of Taranto, including the positions of the Italian warships. They confirmed that the harbor held two *Littorio*-class battleships, the two *Dorias* and the two *Cavours*. All were moored in the *Mar Grande*, the outer harbor, which was somewhat more open than the *Mar Piccolo*, a tight, land-locked anchorage more difficult for torpedo aircraft to attack.

The photos also showed, however, a line of what appeared to be barrage balloons stretched across the target area. The cables hanging beneath the balloons—designed to destroy low-flying aircraft—would have to be avoided by attacking torpedo planes . . . and avoided in the dark. In addition to the forest of anti-aircraft weapons, there were searchlights, both ashore and afloat; the lights posed a real danger: Their beams were easily bright enough to blind the Swordfish aircrews in the middle of their low-level run into the targets. Lyster had to assume—and Italian documents would later confirm—that the base's AA guns were fully manned and ready.

Some good luck the British had: Recent storms had damaged some of the barrage balloons so there were fewer of them to cope with on this night, and the torpedo nets did not cover much of the sea around the anchored Italian ships. There was a shortage of construction material, for one thing, and the Italian admiral in command at Taranto—Campioni—was impatient with the unwieldy nets. Opening them made putting to sea a lengthy and cumbersome process. Believing Cunningham had turned for his homeward trip to Alexandria, Campioni proposed to sail the next morning to shell the British installations at Crete's Suda Bay. Taranto, oddly, possessed no smoke-making equipment, which at least would have obscured the vision of the second wave of British aircraft.

British aerial recon photographed the harbor again on the afternoon of the day set for the strike, the 11th of November—World War I Armistice Day. The photos were taken at only eight thousand feet, and were clear and precise. That afternoon Admiral Cunningham signaled R.A.A. (Rear Admiral Aircraft), asking the critical question: Did the last pictures "give you any doubt as to the possibility of the operation?" And the R.A.A. replied, "I am confident that although hazardous the operation is feasible."

The Taranto show was on.

The task force sailed from Alexandria on November 6, moving west, meeting and covering the vital Malta–Suda Bay convoy. *Illustrious*'s fighters drove off Italian bombers trying to strike the convoy, shooting down two of them, and either drove off or shot down enemy Cant reconnaissance aircraft, keeping the enemy in comparative darkness.

The attacking aircraft would fly in two waves, the first of twelve planes, the second, since the loss of the three Swordfish to contaminated gasoline, of just nine planes. Two Swordfish in each wave carried nine flares each in addition to their bombs: They would light the harbor for the torpedo aircraft and then go on to bomb other targets. There would be no fighter cover.

The assault plan called for the torpedo-carriers to attack from the west, out of darkness, leaving the Italian ships silhouetted against the moon. The carefully dropped flares would enhance the ambient light, making the anchored Italian warships prime targets for the lumbering Swordfish. Although the aircraft had to take off in the gloom before moonrise, they would have moonlight to help them make it back to

Illustrious and get their aircraft, perhaps seriously damaged, back on her deck.

At 8:30 on the night of the 11th of November, sailing at twenty-eight knots, *Illustrious* turned into the wind a few miles off Kabbo Point on the island of Cephalonia (today called Keffalinia), off the west coast of Greece and some 170 miles from the objective. As the green "go" light flashed from Flying Control, the aircraft fitters and riggers dropped flat on the deck and jerked away the wheel-chocks. The pilot of the lead aircraft opened his throttle, then others behind him opened theirs, and the dark deck blossomed with the brilliant little fireflies of engine exhausts.

The first wave roared off into the darkness, led by Lieutenant-Commander Kenneth Williamson, commander of 815 Squadron, with Lt. N. J. Scarlett flying in the rear seat. An hour later the second wave was airborne, led into the night by the commanding officer of 819 Squadron, Lieutenant Commander J. W. Hale.; behind him sat his observer, Lt. G. A. Carline.

None of the attacking aircraft carried its air gunner, his weight and space sacrificed for fuel and range. The observer had to share his cockpit with a sixty-gallon fuel tank. This auxiliary fitting had a nasty tendency to slop gasoline from its overflow spout when the aircraft accelerated into takeoff.

As the first wave of Swordfish took off into the gloom of the Mediterranean night, they carried with them the benediction of Admiral Cunningham to *Illustrious*. "Good luck then to your lads in their enterprise. Their success may well have a most important bearing on the course of the war in the Mediterranean."

It would indeed.

Running into clouds along the way, four aircraft were separated from Williamson's flight. He did not try to rally his scattered aircraft, but pushed on with what he had: five torpedo-carriers, two flare-dropping Swordfish, and a single bomb-carrier. By the time his aircraft appeared over Taranto, the Italians were already alert and firing blindly into the air. The defenders had heard "suspicious noises from the air" about 10:25 p.m., either a Sunderland flying boat on routine reconnaissance or a lost Swordfish that had pushed on ahead alone and reached the target early.

The flare-dropping Swordfish began lighting up the harbor at 11:00 p.m., and the torpedo planes started their runs a quarter of an hour later. The night sky above Taranto was a jungle of tracer, a sky so crowded with flying death that it must have seemed impossible to press home an attack, especially straight and level almost on the surface of the harbor. Through that hail of anti-aircraft fire, the fragile Swordfish bored in, the torpedo aircraft closing on the line of Italian warships silhouetted by the moon and the magnesium flares dropped by their squadron-mates.

They were flying into the fire of twenty-one batteries of 76-millimeter or larger, eighty-four 20-millimeter guns, and more than one hundred other automatic weapons. During this attack and the one to follow by the second wave, the Italians filled the air with steel: almost eighty-six hundred cannon rounds and almost five thousand from heavy machine guns and automatic pom-poms. That does not even count the colossal curtain of machine gun fire put up by the ships themselves.

Through all of this the Swordfish pilots would fly just above the water—one pilot was so low that he dipped a wheel in the harbor—holding a straight line to the target and holding the aircraft level in two planes so that the fish would run straight. The pilot would try to get as close to his target as he could, but he had to be sure to drop beyond three hundred yards, the distance in which the torpedo armed.

Then there was the desperate race to get clear of the harbor, jinking through the mass of tracers—"flaming onions" to the pilots—twisting past the masts and superstructure of Italian ships. As one pilot—Lt. A. R. Maund—described it later:

> *The white balls come scorching across our quarter as we turn and twist over the harbour . . . so close a pattern that I can smell the acrid smoke of their tracer . . . flying the machine close down on the water, wing-tips all but scraping it at every turn, throttle full open and wide back.*

In spite of the hail of missiles flying toward them over the harbor, the Swordfish bored in to drop their fish. Miraculously, only a single aircraft was hit, that of the leader himself. Williamson and Scarlett crash-landed in the harbor, but they had gotten a torpedo into *Cavour* before their Swordfish hit the water. Unhurt, they were picked up by a small boat and became prisoners of war. Two nights after the strike, during an air-raid alert, they were moved to a shelter full of Italian sailors and there they were made welcome, offered cigarettes, and finally serenaded with "Tipperary."

Just before midnight, while the Italians were still blazing away in all directions, the second wave turned in to attack. There were only seven of them—one aircraft had been forced to turn back with mechanical problems and a second was still under repair on *Illustrious* when the second wave flew off. But the two flare-droppers did their work and Lieutenant-Commander Hale led his five torpedo planes in from the northwest. One blew up and disappeared in the night, although its pilot may have dropped his fish before the shell found him. Hale's men got two hits, one on *Littorio*—already hit twice in the first strike—the other on *Duilio*.

Another Swordfish, bombing from only five hundred feet, was rewarded by a large secondary explosion and massive fires from the seaplane base. Lieutenants E. W. Clifford and G. R. M. Going, crew of the plane delayed for repair, insisted on taking off alone and twenty-four minutes late. Pushing on at the best speed their Swordfish would make, they arrived in the middle of the raid and attacked with bombs. The gallantry achieved nothing: They got a hit on cruiser *Trento*, but the bomb failed to detonate. Both men received well-earned DSOs for their determination.

The log of Pilot-Officer J. W. G. Wellham described his wild night over the Italian port:

> *Arrived target midnight. Flew over town and base . . . met barrage balloon at 7000' (prob. Adrift.) dived thro' intense . . . barrage: hit by M.G. bullets . . . strut smashed. Form. Lt. blown off . . . out of control for 500'. Dropped fish on pt. qutr. of "Littorio" prob. hit. Turned to stbd. hit by expl. Breda bullets . . . spars smashed. Got away safely. . . . Results of raid: – 3 battleships out of action . . . not bad!*

Lieutenant-Commander L. J. Kiggell laconically logged his own participation: "attack on Taranto (bag three battleships)."

And so, as the horrified Italians listened to the distant drone of the last departing Swordfish and looked around their devastated harbor, they found that the battleship strength of Mussolini's navy had been suddenly cut in half. Big *Littorio*'s bow was partially underwater; she had taken three torpedoes. Like her, *Duilio*, hit by a single fish, would be out of action for a critical half year. *Cavour*, badly hit, beached, and largely under water, was finished . . . she would never again be fit to put to sea.

Cruiser *Trento* was out of action, damaged by a bomb that had failed to explode but done serious structural damage anyway. Two destroyers had been damaged by the blast force of near-misses. The seaplane base was in ashes. The enormous expenditure of Italian anti-aircraft ordnance accounted for further damage to the port facilities, the town, and to warships hitting each other as the Swordfish roared between them. "A black day," wrote Italian foreign minister Count Ciano in his diary.

British losses amounted to just two aircraft. Williamson and Scarlett were prisoners of the Italians. The other crew—Lieutenants G. W. Bayly and H. J. Slaughter—was simply gone, vanished with their aircraft in a burst of crimson and yellow in the night. Bayly's body was recovered; Slaughter's was never found. Their comrades came home, to *Illustrious*, many of the reliable old stringbags studded with Italian bullet holes . . . but still flying. Before 3:00 a.m. all but the two lost birds were back.

Admiral Lyster later commented privately on the absence of Eagle: "Her fine squadrons (instead of only a few representatives) would have increased the weight of the attack considerably, and I believe would have made it devastating."

He was probably right. Nevertheless, the importance of the victory was obvious. The Italians moved their fleet to more northern ports, making it safer, but also taking it away from any chance of making a sudden sortie in the Med. "By means of the aerial offensive," wrote Italian admiral Romeo Bernotti, *the enemy had achieved results which obliged the nucleus of our naval power to move away from southern water, that is from the area where they were most likely to be employed.*

And the British strike more than evened the odds: Cunningham could now face the reduced Italian battle fleet without his two oldest battleships, *Malaya* and *Ramillies*, which freed up some of his precious destroyers from screening the two big ships.

Moreover, Taranto was not only another plain assertion of British naval prowess over the Italian enemy, but a spectacular demonstration of what even a few well-handled torpedo aircraft could achieve. The Japanese navy studied the raid very closely—for Pearl Harbor was only a year in the future—even sending a naval mission to Taranto to consider firsthand the scene of the British success.

If anybody still doubted the efficacy of aerial torpedoes against shipping in harbor, they had only to consult the record of Royal Navy torpedo attacks during 1940. Including Taranto, thirty-six torpedoes yielded fifteen hits, a respectable 41.8 percent. The average for *all* torpedoes dropped that year, including those dropped at sea, was 36.4, a hit percentage of better than one-third. Naval aviation had arrived with a bang.

Commendation came to Cunningham from King George VI, a warm message the admiral immediately passed to the fleet:

The recent successful operations of the fleet under your command have been a source of pride and gratification to all at home. Please convey my warm congratulations to the med. Fleet and in particular to the F.A.A. on their brilliant exploit against the Italian warships at Taranto.

More congratulations came in from RAF Station Gosport, where much research work on torpedoes and training of torpedo pilots had been done. There was even a wire from Vickers-Armstrong, the builders of *Illustrious*, and from the yard that built her at Barrow-In-Furness. And for the ship's complement of the carrier, as she rejoined the main force, three flags jumped to the top of the flagship's signal hoist. It was only four words, but to those who knew Cunningham, it was the highest praise possible: "Illustrious. Manouvre well executed."

Which left Pridham-Wippel's raid into Otranto Strait, which was aimed at disrupting Italian resupply convoys running out of Otranto, Brindisi, and Bari, across the Adriatic to Greece. With Greece fighting to repel Italian invasion, interdiction of the Italian resupply routes would be a material help to the Greek military. And in bright moonlight, at the northernmost end of their search pattern up the Adriatic, destroyer *Mohawk* spotted an Italian convoy, running without lights toward the Italian port of Brindisi.

Signaling to her consorts, *Mohawk* opened fire, hitting a big Italian torpedo boat sailing with a destroyer as part of the escort. Within the next half hour, in a chaotic night action, four merchantmen were sunk and a fifth badly damaged, in spite of the trouble British gunners had in laying their guns against the blinding flash of their own muzzle-blasts. Royal Navy ships did not at that time have "flashless" powder.

Before noon on the 12th, the Otranto Strait force was back with Cunningham's force. It had suffered neither casualties nor damage, and *Illustrious*'s Fulmars had shot down another three "Mama help mes" on the way back. Admiral Lyster at first planned a second strike for the night of the 12th, and *Illustrious* had assembled a fifteen-plane strike force. Hearing this, one British pilot is said to have commented that even the Light Brigade "only had to do it once." But later in the day, the weather deteriorated and the operation was scrubbed. At 6:00 p.m. Cunningham turned for home—Alexandria.

On the 14th the *Egyptian Mail* headlined jubilantly, "Smashing Blow Struck At Italian Fleet," and the *Daily Telegraph*, reporting both the victory at Taranto and the hammering of the Italian convoy in the Straits of Otranto, quoted Winston Churchill as he rose to address the House of Commons on the preceding night:

I have some news for the House. It is good news. The Royal Navy has struck a crippling blow at the Italian Fleet (Prolonged cheers) . . . I feel it my duty to bring this glorious episode—(cheers)—to the immediate notice of the House. As a result of a determined and highly successful attack, which reflects the greatest honour on the Fleet Air Arm, only three of the Italian battleships remain effective.

Taranto was an astonishing triumph for the lumbering Swordfish, but not her first or her last. It was a Swordfish torpedo that jammed the rudder of super-battleship *Bismarck*, keeping her circling until Royal Navy men-of-war could close in and send her to the bottom of the Atlantic. "It was incredible," said a German survivor, "to see such obsolete-looking planes having the nerve to attack a fire-spitting mountain like the *Bismarck*."

In July of 1940 a Swordfish mission against Libya's Bomba Bay had sunk two Italian submarines, a submarine tender, and a destroyer. And a Swordfish from HMS *Warspite*, spotting for the battleship's guns over Norway's Ofot Fjord, shared in the destruction of seven big German fleet destroyers. The same Swordfish bombed and sank a U-boat the same day.

Later, Swordfish would fly hundreds of anti-submarine missions from escort carriers covering British convoys. With a much-improved thousand-mile range, fitted with radar and carrying depth charges and rockets, they were remarkably effective against the *Kriegsmarine*'s *unterseebooten*. Flying in all kinds of weather from escort carriers and MACs—Merchant Aircraft Carriers—converted cargo vessels and tankers, they usually worked at night, twenty-five miles or more ahead of a convoy. Swordfish made fifteen solo U-boat kills, and shared responsibility for another ten with other aircraft and surface vessels. Malta-based Swordfish flying against Italian North African convoys sank an average of fifty thousand tons of shipping each month.

The subsequent history of the daring Taranto aircrew has its sad side, inevitable in a long, brutal war. *Illustrious* was bombed and badly damaged in the Med, but she would survive to fight again. When the war ended she was serving in the Far East with five of her sisters, launching her aircraft against the enemy, in this case the Japanese.

As for the surviving Taranto raiders, two died when the wings of their venerable Swordfish came off during a dive-bombing attack. Another was killed during an enemy attack on the auxiliary carrier in which he was serving, and still another was killed flying out of Alexandria.

Four more were shot down and killed in subsequent operations, one as a night-fighter out of England, a second while flying against enemy shipping out of Malta, a third attacking enemy installations on the Greek island of Leros, and another flying from HMS *Formidable*, when his fighter collided with a German aircraft.

Five flying officers were killed aboard *Illustrious* during the January 1941 German attack, and another badly burned. Still another lost a leg in the raid, but remained on active duty and rose to the rank of commander. The rest survived the war, and many of them served on in the Navy. One, Lt. H. R. B. Janvrin, rose to the rank of vice-admiral. The sole Marine aviator on the raid, Capt. O. Patch, later a major, won the DSO in addition to his Taranto DSC. An obvious glutton for dangerous service, he went on to serve with 40 Commando later in the war.

Several venerable Swordfish are still flying, notably with the Fleet Air Arm Historical Flight in the West Country of England. Along with other venerable aircraft, they are flown by officer pilots out of the Royal Navy Air Station at Yeovilton in Somerset.

Chapter Thirty-Four

Graceful Lady

When Enola Gay *Brought the Fires of Hell to Japan*

As World War II wound down in the Pacific, American planners wrestled with the logical last act. To put an end to Japan's military operations, it would be logical and necessary to invade her home islands. Anybody who had fought the Japanese knew what that would mean: last-ditch fighting, massive military casualties on both sides, colossal civilian casualties, and material damage beyond calculation.

Estimates ranged as high as more than a million western casualties and perhaps twenty times that number of Japanese deaths, many of which would inevitably be women and children. World War II had been a long, hard road: solid years of long casualty lists, rationing, and grief. Now there would inevitably be more agony in this final act, coming on top of all the misery and bloodshed already suffered by the Allies at the hands of these arrogant worshippers of *Bushido*, the way of the warrior. This last act seemed to many weary people to be an unnecessary sacrifice unless it was the only way to end the war.

But there was another way known only to a comparative few, a way to end this long and bloody war other than endless bombardment from the air or the long-planned invasion of Japan—Operation Downfall it was appropriately called—with all the attendant bloodshed. Downfall would necessarily involve many western casualties—maybe as many as a million—and take a very long time; the western Allies ached for peace. The United States had been at war since December of 1941; England, the

British Commonwealth nations, and the empire had been at war since the autumn of 1939.

And there was another factor that played a powerful role in the thinking of people in the west. Japan had committed well-publicized atrocities virtually without number, and had attacked the United States without warning and while Japan's "peace emissaries" were in Washington, DC. These ugly things were not easily forgotten, so there was little of the milk of human kindness in western hearts. Rather, the average American thought—and said—"you started this, you so-and-sos; now we'll finish it, any way we have to."

And so the thoughts of the Allied command turned to a super-weapon, very secret and long in development by the United States and Great Britain. Innocently known as the Manhattan Project in its formative years, it would be popularly known as the atomic bomb when news of it was finally released, and the world would never be the same again.

President Franklin Delano Roosevelt had passed away in April of 1945, and now Vice President Harry Truman sat in the White House. "The buck stops here" was his slogan, and just now he faced the biggest buck ever confronted by an American president, by any head of state, for that matter. Truman knew something about war; he had commanded an artillery battery in Europe after America had entered World War I. He was also a devout Christian.

On his mind and conscience now was the colossal decision whether to use the atomic bomb against Japan. And after much agonizing he decided to use this fearsome weapon, but only after a demand by the Allies for surrender, immediate and unconditional. The Japanese weren't having any of that; they had some two million troops under arms in Japan, and the tradition of *Bushido* was still very much alive. Surrender was still considered dishonorable, and death for the emperor an honorable and desirable thing. The Japanese also feared that unconditional surrender would mean the loss of their beloved emperor, the "Son of Heaven."

And so the die was cast. Truman gave his orders—as he said, the most difficult thing he had ever had to do—and the bomb's components were delivered to the Marianas island of Tinian, part of them flown in, and in part delivered in a lead-lined steel box locked to the deck in the captain's cabin of cruiser USS *Indianapolis*. Once the parts were delivered, the bomb was assembled, and on August 6 sleek B-29 *Enola Gay* took off from the Marianas with the future of the world in her bomb bay. She traveled in company with two other B-29s, *The Great Artiste* and prophetically named *Necessary Evil*, and she was headed for the island of Hokkaido, and the city of Hiroshima.

Enola Gay had gotten her name in the week before the raid, named for the mother of the plane commander, Col. Paul W. Tibbets Jr. The mission commander, Navy captain William Parsons, armed their deadly cargo, called "Little Boy" (he waited to do it in flight as a safety measure), and the safeties came off the bomb about half an hour from the target. *Enola Gay* and Little Boy parted company 31,060 feet above the city of Hiroshima, and the bomb took forty-three seconds to reach its ideal detonation height of 1,968 feet.

And the world changed forever.

The blast from Little Boy and the firestorm that followed destroyed some 69 percent of Hiroshima's buildings and damaged many more, and killed seventy to eighty thousand people, about twenty thousand of them soldiers. There was a desolate wasteland about a mile across where the center of the city had once stood, and the vast increase in illness and death from radiation sickness was still to come.

Enola Gay landed on Tinian to find a considerable crowd waiting, including a large number of reporters and photographers. Tibbets was the first man to step down from the aircraft, and was awarded the Distinguished Service Cross on the spot.

Just three days later B-29 *Bock's Car* dropped a similar weapon on the city of Nagasaki, again inflicting enormous casualties. Most important of all, on the 14th Japan surrendered.

There was some disapproval of the president's decision of course, including some senior military officers who had good reasons for their opinions, and a variety of academics and other civilians who didn't. Over the years Truman has been both widely praised for his decision, but also excoriated for it, called a racist and a murderer, mostly by people whose knowledge of the terrible options Truman faced is either scanty or nonexistent, who couldn't have told you what or where Tinian was.

Nobody knows what would have happened without the dropping of Little Boy and his single successor, but one thing at least is crystal clear. After those two cataclysmic demonstrations of western power, the war stopped almost instantly, saving hundreds of thousands, perhaps millions of lives, and destruction beyond imagining.

President Truman was right.

Afterword

THERE IS MUCH LEFT TO SAY ABOUT THE AIR WAR, MUCH THAT SPEAKS of high courage and stamina, guts and skill, triumph and tragedy. For those things are an integral part of war generally, a terrible, wonderful, ugly happening unique to the human experience. They are also part of that war that is fought in the sky, and the human experience that goes with war in a new dimension.

We have been able to do no more than touch on the story of airfighting in the two world wars, and any mention at all of later wars—Korea and Vietnam in particular—will have to wait for another volume, or maybe even two. So also will stories of transport aircraft and hospital planes, which both require of their crews the same courage, enterprise, and skill as the combat aircraft do, except, as an Air Force acquaintance who flew transports once said, "you can't shoot back."

We'll also leave for a later volume the wonders and miseries that accompany parachute assaults, for they too are a part of war and likely to remain so. Hostile folks are likely to shoot at you when you come to jump down their throats, and they sure will when you land. But paratroops will keep right on jumping, for one reason, as author Smith can testify, simply to get out of the airplane and descend to someplace where you can get out of the damned harness that's been cutting into your body for hours.

Remember when you read our tales that they're about people who stood between civilized nations and chaos. They happened more than half a century ago, but one thing you can always be sure of: The arrogant tyrants and murderous religious fanatics are out there waiting, just as they always have and they always will be.

And there will always be those who oppose anything they think might disturb their pleasant status quo or endanger their own precious hides, like the protester in a dirty tee shirt who shouted at author Smith during the Vietnam War, "there's not a f—— thing that's worth going to war over."

Yes, there is.

The protester's attitude is not going to go away anytime real soon, for it is widely prevalent, even fashionable, today, especially in over-educated folks who have had things good and comfortable all their lives. They assume that their world will continue to be beautiful without having to concern themselves with such nasty, mundane things as duty and sacrifice.

The men and women who wear the uniforms of our country and her allies are all that stand between us and our families and Armageddon.

They are our national treasure.

Bibliography

Ashcroft, Michael, Marshal of the RAF. *Heroes of the Skies*. London: Headline, 2012.
———. *Victoria Cross Heroes*. London: Headline, 2006.
Bowyer, Chaz. *Albert Ball, V.C.* Manchester, UK: Crecy, 2008.
Boyington, "Pappy" (Col. Gregory Boyington, USMC Ret.). *Baa, Baa Black Sheep*. New York: Putnam, 1958.
Brickhill, Paul. *The Dambusters*. London: Evans, 1961.
———. *Reach for the Sky*. London: Cassell, 2004.
Bryant, Sir Arthur. *Triumph in the West*. London: Collins, 1959.
———. *The Turn of the Tide*. London: Collins, 1959.
Churchill, Sir Winston. *Closing the Ring*. London: Cassell, 1951.
———. *The Hinge of Fate*. London: Cassell, 1950.
———. *The Gathering Storm*. London: Houghton Mifflin, 1948.
Clark, Alan. *Aces High*. London: Cassell, 1999.
Cooke, David C. *Sky Battle: 1914–1918*. New York: Norton, 1917.
Cooper, Bryan, and John Batchelor. *Fighter*. New York: Scribner's, n.d.
Craig, William. *Enemy at the Gates*. New York: Ballantine, 1968.
Ford, Daniel. *Flying Tigers: Claire Chennault and the American Volunteer Group*. Washington, DC, and London: Smithsonian Institution Press, 1991.
Franks, Norman. *American Aces of World War I*. Oxford, UK: Osprey, 2001.
Fuller, J. F. C. *The Conduct of War, 1798–1961*. Boston, MA: De Capo Press, 1992.
Gabreski, Francis, and Carl Molesworth. *Gabby: A Fighter Pilot's Life*. Atglen, PA: Schiffer Publishing, Ltd., 1998.
Galland, Adolf. *The First and the Last*. New York: Bantam, 1978.
Gamble, Bruce D. *Black Sheep One: The Life of Gregory "Pappy" Boyington*. Novato, CA: Presidio Press, 2000.
———. *The Black Sheep: The Definitive Account of Marine Fighting Squadron 214 in World War II*. Novato, CA: Presidio Press, 1998.
Gibbons, Floyd. *The Red Knight of Germany*. Garden City, NY: Garden City Publishing, 1927.
Guttman, Jon. *SE5a vs Albatros DV*. Oxford, UK: Osprey, 2009.

———. *Sopwith Camel.* Oxford, UK: Osprey, 2012.

Hart, Peter. *Aces Falling.* London: Phoenix, 2008.

Herris, Jack, and Bob Pearson. *Aircraft of World War I.* London: Amber Books, 2010.

Hoyt, Edwin P. *McCampbell's Heroes: The Story of the U.S. Navy's Most Celebrated Carrier Fighters of the Pacific War.* New York: Van Nostrand Reihold Company, 1983.

Jablonski, Edward. *Airwar.* London: Doubleday, 1971.

Jane's Fighting Ships of World War II. New York: Creston Books/Random House, 1989.

Johnson, J. J. E. *Full Circle.* New York: Bantam, 1980.

———. *Wing Leader.* Manchester, UK: Crecy, 2000.

Jones, Ian. *King of Airfighters.* Drexel Hill, PA: Casemate, 2009.

Keegan, John. *The Price of Admiralty.* London: Hutchinson, 1988.

Kemp, Peter. *History of the Royal Navy.* Worthing, UK: Littlehampton, 1969.

Konstam, Angus. *Taranto, 1940.* Oxford, UK: Osprey, 2015.

Lawson, Ted W. *Thirty Seconds Over Tokyo.* New York: Pocket Star, 2002.

Lee, Arthur Gould. *Open Cockpit.* London: Grub Street, 2013.

Longstreet, Stephen. *The Canvas Falcons.* New York: Barnes & Noble, 1995.

Lyal, Gavin. *The War in the Air.* New York: William Morrow, 1968.

McIntyre Donald. *The Naval War Against Hitler.* New York: Charles Scribner's Sons, 1971.

Munson, Kenneth. *Fighters 1914-19.* Suffolk, UK: MacMillan, 1968.

Pardoe, Blaine L. *Terror of the Autumn Skies: The Story of Frank Luke, America's Rogue Ace of World War I.* New York: Skyhorse Publishing, 2008.

Park, Edwards. *Fighters* New York: Barnes & Noble, 1990.

This England. The Register of the Victoria Cross. London:This England, 1981.

Reynolds, Quentin. *They Fought for the Sky.* New York: Bantam, 1968.

Roe, Frederic Gordon. *The Bronze Cross.* London: P. R. Gawthorn, Ltd., 1945.

Ross, John F. *Enduring Courage: Ace Pilot Eddie Rickenbacker and the Dawn of the Age of Speed.* New York: St. Martin's Press, 2014.

Shores, Christopher. *British and Empire Aces of World War I.* Oxford, UK: Osprey, 2001.

Smith, Robert Barr. *Men at War.* New York: Avon, 1997.

———. *To the Last Cartridge.* New York: Avon, 1994; London: Robinson (UK), 1996.

Smith, S. E. *The United States Marine Corps in WW II.* New York: Random House, 1969.

Stokes, Doug. *Paddy Finucane, Fighter Ace.* Manchester, UK: Crecy Publishing Limited, 1992.

Time-Lif. *The Luftwaffe.* Alexandria, VA: Time-Life, 1982.

Whitehouse, Arch. *Heroes and Legends of World War I.* New York: Doubleday, 1964.

———. *Heroes of the Sunlit Sky.* New York: Modern Library Editions Publishing Company, 1967.

Widner, Emil J. *Military Observation Balloons.* Lexington, KY: Read Books Ltd., 2013.

Wukovits, John. *Flying Aces.* San Diego, CA: Lucent Books, 2002.

Index

Ace, explanation of, 58, 90
Adamson, Hans (Col.), 53
Adlertag, 217–20
AEF. *See* American Expeditionary Forces
A Flight, 208–11
Ajax, HMS (ship), 265, 268
Albacore, USS (ship), 259
Albatros (plane), 16, 33, 40, 58; D.II, 90; D.III, 82, 90; for von Richthofen, 83, 90
Alexander, Robert (Lt.), 152
All Blacks. *See* No. 10 Naval Squadron
Allied powers. *See* America; Britain
Allmenroeder, Karl, 40
America, 52–54; AEF, 45, 56; AVG, 145–49; balloons for, 64–65, 73–74, 76; Black Sheep Squadron, 149–54; Boyington for, 143–57; CAMCO in, 145–46; Congressional Medal of Honor for, 155–56, 162, 185–86, 200–201, 253; Escadrille Americaine, 45–47; 5th Balloon Company, 73–74; Fifth Air Force, 182; Fighter Squadron 15, 197, 201; 1st Marine Aircraft Wing, 149–50; 1st Pursuit Group, 57, 59, 71–76; 1st Squadron, 146–48; Flying Tigers, 143, 146–49, 157; Foss for, 153, 161–64; Gabreski for, 223–29; against Japan, 249–54, 257–60, 283–86; Legion of Merit for, 169; Luke for, 66, 71–77; MacArthur for, 53, 55, 185; in Mariana Island Chain, 257–60; Marshall for, 53; McCampbell for, 195–201; 94th Aero Pursuit Squadron, 57; 94th Aero Squadron, 47, 59; Pearl Harbor attack against, 52–53, 147, 196, 225, 276; Pershing